Prayer Companion

A Treasury of Personal Meditation

Judith Lawrence

Path Books

A LIGHT TO MY PATH

Path Books
an imprint of ABC Publishing
Anglican Book Centre
600 Jarvis Street
Toronto, Ontario M4Y 2J6

Calligraphy by Judith Lawrence.

Cover design by Saskia Rowley.

Acknowledgements

Anam Cara: A Book of Celtic Wisdom. Copyright 1997 by John O'Donohue.
Used by permission of HarperCollins Publishers, Inc.

The Artist's Way. Copright 1992 by Julia Cameron. Used by permission of Jeremy
P. Tarcher, a division of Penguin Putnam Inc.

Community and Growth by Jean Vanier. Published and copyright 1979 and
1989 by Darton, Longman and Todd Limited. Used by pemission of the publishers. Paulist Press (U.S. and Canada)

Mother Teresa: In My Own Words. Copyright 1996 by José Luis Gonzalez-
Balado. Used by permission of Hodder and Stoughton Limited.

New Seeds of Contemplation by Thomas Merton. Copyright 1961 by The Abbey of Gethsemani, Inc. Used by permission of New Directions Publishing
Corp.

N.R.S.V. The scripture quotations contained herein (unless otherwise noted)
are from the New Revised Standard Version Bible, copyright © 1989 by the
Division of Christian Education of the National Council of the Churches of
Christ in the U.S.A. Used by permission. All rights reserved.

Canadian Cataloguing in Publication Data

Lawrence, Judith, 1937-
   Prayer Companion: a treasury of personal meditation
ISBN 1-55126-319-X
1. Prayer-books. I. Title.
BV260.L38 2000   242'.8   C00-932810-6

To my sisters
and companions in Christ,
Helen, Maria, and Penny

Every scribe who has been trained
for the kingdom of heaven is like
the master of a household
who brings out of his treasure
what is new and what is old

Matthew 13:52.

Table of Contents

Introduction

When I started to write this book a few years ago, I planned to present, in alphabetical order, prayers that had been helpful to me and to share them with the reader. But it has turned out to be more than this. It is a book of Bible readings, prayers, and meditations that have brought me closer to God. I share them with you in the hope that you can use them as places from which to jump into your own prayer life.

The book shows what I have understood from certain Bible passages and psalm verses, and allows you to develop your own thoughts and meditations. Your interpretation may be totally different from mine, but this is natural. We each have our own unique friendship with God.

Throughout this book there are personal prayer suggestions as well as creative ideas to enhance your prayer life. I am not offering any "must-do's" or prescribing a certain number of hours or minutes that you should devote to prayer. Everyone is different, and God asks different things of each of us at different times in life.

In your daily life, you have time for one thing and not another, or you are inclined to do one thing and not another. It is the same in your prayer life. On some days you will have time to devote to a certain prayer routine, but on others not. Or you will be inclined now to one method, now to another.

I suggest that none of this will matter if you recognize that your whole life is a prayer. You can talk and listen to God through every part of your day, practising the presence of God as Brother

Lawrence did in the mid-seventeenth century, by continually sharing his thoughts with God.

> *We should establish ourselves in a sense of God's Presence by continually conversing with Him.... We should feed and nourish our souls with high notions of God; which would yield us great joy in being devoted to Him* (Brother Lawrence, The Practice of the Presence of God).

Instead of feeling pressure to maintain a certain prayer routine when it is no longer possible because of time restrictions, or no longer helpful to your spiritual growth, you can experience the freedom to pray at all times. God is with you always, and you can talk to God at any moment. Whenever you realize that you have forgotten God's presence with you, or you have not spoken with him for a little while, a prayer such as the Agnus Dei, or the Jesus Prayer, or an arrow prayer can bring you back to an awareness of God within you. Having reminded yourself of God's presence, you can carry on with your work or play with a smile in your heart. Any chore will seem lighter, and any play will be more joyous.

Sometimes we need a little assistance. There are days when, no matter how hard you try, you just cannot get started; or if you get started, you cannot concentrate. This book is set up so that you can dip into it anywhere and find some prayer or thought to help you to enter God's presence. Or you can read it through and allow yourself to be led to God through the prayers, readings, and meditations in their alphabetical order.

However you use the book, I hope that it helps to bring you blessing and enjoyment in your prayer life.

ACTS

Adoration, Confession, Thanksgiving, and Supplication

ACTS is an acronym for Adoration, Confession, Thanksgiving, and Supplication. It is a simple aid to memory, so that you can include each of these elements in your prayers. When you have a lot on your mind and can't seem to concentrate on prayer, ACTS may enable you to bring yourself back to the point before you became distracted.

ACTS can be used at any time — as an opening to meditation, as a beginning to a church service, or during the day when you need to remind yourself of God's presence. Sometimes it may be helpful to recall words from scripture or worship. At other times you may prefer to make up your own words. Here are some phrases that I've found helpful.

Prayer suggestions for adoration

ᴄᴠ "I praise you, O God, I acknowledge you to be the Lord. All the earth worships you, the Father everlasting."

ᴄᴠ "I worship you, I glorify you, I bow down before you, O Lord."

ᴄᴠ "I adore you, O God: Creator, Redeemer, and Holy Spirit."

ᴄᴠ Any words of worship or praise can be used in adoration; for example, words from a familiar hymn, the Gloria, the psalms:

Praise the Lord from the heavens;
praise him in the heights!
Praise him, all his angels;
praise him, all his host!
Praise him, sun and moon;
praise him, all you shining stars! (Psalm 148:1–3)

ᴄᴠ Try writing your own verses to add to these. Something like:

Praise him, all you tulips and daffodils.
Praise him, all you flowers.
Praise him, all you sparrows and wrens.
Praise him, all you birds of song.

Prayer suggestions for confession

ᴄᴠ "Lord, I am sorry for the things I did (today/this week) that offended or injured other people, the earth, or myself." (Then it helps to be specific: I'm sorry for making Joan wait because I was in a bad mood. I'm sorry for yelling at Robert.

Rather than: I'm sorry for being mean.) "Lord, forgive me; help me to put things right; help me not to do this again."

- ❧ If today you feel that you have nothing specific to confess, there is no need to dredge up a misdeed. Just thank God for guiding you.

Prayer suggestions for thanksgiving

- ❧ "Lord, I thank you for the many blessings you have given to me. Especially I want to thank you for ..." (Again it helps to be specific: people, home, food, someone's smile, a shoulder to cry on...)
- ❧ Most of us are unaware of all that we've received in the course of a day. but if you start to make a list, you'll be amazed at all the things you have been given.
- ❧ Try keeping a gratitude journal.

Prayer suggestions for supplication

- ❧ "God, who said through your son Jesus, 'Ask, and it will be given you; search, and you will find; knock, and the door will be opened for you,' I pray you now to give me these special blessings ..." (And again, it helps to be specific: name the things you need for yourself, your friends and family, the world.)

Pray for strength in a special undertaking.
Pray for the ability to be patient or to bear an illness.

Pray for understanding in dealing with difficulties
   you are experiencing.
Pray for healing of rifts in a relationship.
Pray for peace in the world, for relief of famine.

∾ Sometimes your needs are met before you know them, and only later do you see the reasons for a particular trial. For instance, you may lose your job, on the surface not a good thing, but an opportunity to work at something you've always wanted to do may present itself, and you are free to take it.

Advent
Preparing for Christmas

The word *advent* means arrival or coming, usually of someone important. In the church it is the beginning of the year's cycle and a time of preparation for the birth of Christ. Advent is not as rigorous a preparation for Christmas as Lent is for Easter, but it has the same purpose — to prepare minds and hearts for the big event.

The season of Advent begins on the Sunday nearest to the Feast of St. Andrew, which is celebrated on November 30. There are always four Sundays in Advent, though the number of days in the fourth week of Advent varies. The secular world is well into Christmas celebrations by the beginning of December, and most of us are caught up in this — the shopping, the parties, the gifts, the food. But if you would like to do something special to prepare yourself spiritually for the day of Christ's birth, here are some ideas you can follow.

Prayer suggestions

❧ Spend a few minutes each day to

read the passages of scripture set out by the church or as suggested later in this Advent section,
read the psalms appointed for the day or the week,
jot down in a notebook verses or words that strike you while you read,
meditate on their meaning for your life.

❧ This quiet time is like taking a deep spiritual breath in the midst of the secular hurry and bustle of the Christmas season.

Creative ideas

Use an Advent Wreath to celebrate the season. You can do this whether you are alone or with others.

An Advent Wreath consists of a circle of greenery — you can buy one or make your own. Place four purple or blue candles into the greenery to represent the four Sundays of Advent, and one white candle in the centre of the circle, to represent Christ's birth.

The first week you light one purple candle, the second week you light two, and so on, until the four candles are lit.

On Christmas Day you light the four purple candles and the white candle to celebrate Christ's coming into the world and into your heart.

A scripture reading, a spoken prayer, or a silent meditation can accompany the lighting of these candles. The time can be as short or as long as you wish.

You might listen to some music during your Advent lighting ceremony and then sit in an attitude of quiet expectancy.

Meditative thoughts

In Advent most of us are already experiencing the season of Christmas in our everyday life — the shops and streets are decorated; there are Christmas parties and festive celebrations.

Many people feel stress at this time. For some the stress comes from having too much to do and being overwhelmed by the demands of family and friends. For others it comes from having nothing to do. People who live alone, with no family or friends to share this season, may feel lonely and left out of the happy times they imagine others are experiencing.

If you are suffering from stress or loneliness at this time, you may find it helpful to meditate on Mary, the mother of Jesus.

∽ What stress did Mary feel as she waited for Christ's birth and faced the unknown? What fear and anxiety did she feel? How could she explain the situation to Joseph?

∽ How did Mary maintain her serenity? Consider her reliance on family — Joseph and her cousin Elizabeth. Consider her trust that God would make it right for her and Joseph and the baby.

~ Does her response suggest ways to deal with your own time of stress or loneliness? If you are overwhelmed by too much to do, are there friends or family who can help? If you are lonely, can you make the first move and reach out to someone else?

The O Antiphons are said at Evening Prayer, before and after the Magnificat, during the last seven days before the Vigil of Christmas. They are a tradition in the church dating back to the seventh or eighth century, and are said by some Monastic Orders and others who use the Breviary for their daily order of prayers.

They begin on December 17 or, for those using an ancient English Order, on December 16. In this latter tradition there are eight antiphons instead of seven, the last one being a title for Mary while the first seven are titles given to Christ.

It has been pointed out that the first letters of the Latin titles spelt backwards give the Latin phrase "ero cras." Its English meaning is "I shall be there tomorrow."

O Sapientia: Wisdom   December 17 [16]
O Wisdom, coming forth from the mouth of the Most High,
and reaching mightily from one end of the earth to the other,
ordering all things well:
Come and teach us the way of prudence.

O Adonai: Lord   December 18 [17]
O Adonai, and leader of the house of Israel,
who appeared to Moses in the fire of the burning bush
and gave him the law on Sinai:
Come and redeem us with an outstretched arm.

O Radix: Root of Jesse   December 19 [18]
O Root of Jesse, standing as a sign to the people,
before whom kings shall shut their mouths,
and whom the nations shall seek:
Come and deliver us and do not delay.

O Clavis: Key of David   December 20 [19]
O Key of David, and sceptre of the house of Israel,
who opens and no one can shut,
who shuts and no one can open:
Come, and bring the prisoners from the prison house,
those who dwell in darkness and the shadow of death.

O Oriens: Dawn   December 21 [20]
O Daystar, splendour of light eternal,
and sun of righteousness:
Come and enlighten those who dwell in darkness and the shadow
of death.

O Rex: King of Nations   December 22 [21]
O King of the nations, and their desire;
the cornerstone making both one:
Come and save us, whom you formed from the dust.

O Emmanuel   December 23 [22]
O Emmanuel, our King and Lawgiver,
the desire of all nations and their Saviour:
Come and save us, O Lord our God.

Virgin of Virgins   December [23]
O Virgin of Virgins, how shall this be?
For before you no one was seen who was like you,
nor shall there be anyone after.
Daughters of Jerusalem, why marvel at me?
What you behold is a divine mystery.

Advent 1

In the week of Advent 1, the prophet Isaiah foretells the coming of the Messiah:

> *The people who walked in darkness have seen a great*
> *light; those who lived in a land of deep darkness — on*
> *them light has shined.... For a child has been born for us,*
> *a son given to us; authority rests upon his shoulders; and*
> *he is named Wonderful Counsellor* (Isaiah 9:2, 6).

Prayer suggestions

- Close your eyes and feel the darkness around you. See Jesus, the babe of Bethlehem, as a light before your eyes, the light of the world.
- Feel the happiness that this light brings into your life. Thank God for sending Jesus into the world to lighten your darkness and the darkness of the world.
- In the dark of winter, light some candles and meditate on Christ, the light of the world.

Advent 2

In the week of Advent 2, John the Baptist, Jesus' cousin, speaks of the coming of the Messiah:

> John the Baptist appeared in the wilderness of Judea, proclaiming, "Repent, for the kingdom of heaven has come near." This is the one of whom the prophet Isaiah spoke when he said, "The voice of one crying out in the wilderness: 'Prepare the way of the Lord, make his paths straight'" (Matthew 3:1–3).

Advent is a time of spiritual housekeeping, a time to examine your life. It gives you an opportunity to rethink or repent, to prepare or repair, a path to God.

Prayer suggestions

- Choose one thing you would like to change in your life, and write down a plan of action to enable you to make this change.
- Ask God to help you to make this change in your life.

Advent 3

In the week of Advent 3, Jesus reassures John the Baptist that he is the Messiah:

> When John heard in prison what the Messiah was doing, he sent word by his disciples and said to him, "Are you the

one who is to come, or are we to wait for another?" Jesus
answered them, "Go and tell John what you hear and see:
the blind receive their sight, the lame walk, the lepers are
cleansed, the deaf hear, the dead are raised, and the poor
have good news brought to them. And blessed is anyone
who takes no offense at me" (Matthew 11:2–6).

Even those who seem secure in their faith, like John the Baptist, have times of doubt and need to be reassured.

Prayer suggestions

- ∽ Tell God that sometimes you don't understand why things are happening as they are. Ask to be shown how God is working in the world and in your life.
- ∽ Look at the past week. Name one good thing that has happened to you or to someone else.
- ∽ Thank God for this good thing that strengthens your faith.

Advent 4

In the week of Advent 4, the Angel Gabriel tells Mary that she will conceive a child and the child shall be called Jesus:

The angel said to her, "Do not be afraid, Mary, for you
have found favour with God. And now, you will conceive
in your womb and bear a son, and you will name him
Jesus" (Luke 1:30–31).

Mary must have been overwhelmed by God's call to be the mother of the Saviour. But the angel who gave her the news of the approaching birth of the Messiah also tells her not to be afraid. God chose her because she had found favour with God, and promised to support and lead her every step of the way.

Sometimes it may seem that God asks you to do more than you are able. But God asks you because you have found favour with God, and promises to support you and give you strength to carry out what has been asked of you.

Prayer suggestions

∽ Ask God for strength and courage to accept his vocation for you.
∽ Ask God to help you not to be afraid.

Agnus Dei
Christ the sacrificial Lamb

The prayer Agnus Dei is from the Latin, meaning "Lamb of God." These words were used by John the Baptist to describe Jesus:

> *The next day John saw Jesus coming toward him and declared, "Here is the Lamb of God who takes away the sin of the world" (John 1:29).*

Centuries ago these words were made into a short litany to be said just before the distribution of bread and wine at the Eucharist. The litany compares Christ to a sacrificial lamb because he died to redeem our humanity. To the first two phrases were added a plea for mercy; to the third, a plea for peace. When we pray this litany, we are asking Christ to have mercy on us for the burdens we bear — pain, sorrow, guilt, fear — and to be with us and give us peace. It is especially appropriate to say this litany just before we receive communion, but it can be helpful anytime that we wish to enter the presence of Christ.

> *O Lamb of God, who takes away the sin of the world,*
> *have mercy upon us.*
> *O Lamb of God, who takes away the sin of the world,*
> *have mercy upon us.*
> *O Lamb of God, who takes away the sin of the world,*
> *grant us your peace.*

In the Old Testament it was required that the sacrificial lamb should be without blemish:

> *If the offering is a sacrifice of well-being, if you offer an*
> *animal of the herd, whether male or female, you shall*
> *offer one without blemish before the Lord* (Leviticus 3:1).

The purpose of the offering was to cleanse the person making the offering.

> *The priest shall take one of the lambs, and offer it as a*
> *guilt offering … the priest shall offer the sin offering, to*
> *make atonement for the one to be cleansed … and he shall*
> *be clean* (Leviticus 14:12, 19, 20).

In the writing of prophet Isaiah, we see the beginning of the bridge between the old and new covenants:

> *All we like sheep have gone astray; we have all turned to*
> *our own way, and the Lord has laid on him the iniquity of*
> *us all. He was oppressed, and he was afflicted, yet he did*
> *not open his mouth; like a lamb that is led to the slaugh-*
> *ter, and like a sheep that before its shearers is silent, so he*
> *did not open his mouth* (Isaiah 53:6, 7).

Jesus freely offered to act as a sacrificial lamb to take away our sins and make us pure.

> *You know that you were ransomed from the futile ways*
> *inherited from your ancestors, not with perishable things*
> *like silver or gold, but with the precious blood of Christ, like*
> *that of a lamb without defect or blemish* (1 Peter 1:18, 19).

We are assured that God does have mercy upon us, because God

> *gave his only Son, so that everyone who believes in him*
> *may not perish but may have eternal life* (John 3:16).

Prayer suggestions

- ∾ Think of Jesus offering himself as a sacrifice for all humanity. Give thanks for Christ's sacrifice.
- ∾ Accept Christ's mercy with confidence. Give thanks for his
  gift of mercy and be at peace.

Angelus
God in our daily work

Traditionally, the prayers of the Angelus are said during the ringing of church bells at 6:00 a.m., 12 noon, and 6:00 p.m. In
response to the bells, all those who hear may recite the Angelus,
a memorial of the birth of Christ on earth as a human being.
Through the incarnation, God in Christ joins us in earthly labour. The Angelus may be said anytime that we want to recall
the presence of Christ in our lives — wherever we are, whatever
we do. During the first set of three bells, pray:

> *The angel of the Lord brought good news to Mary,*
> *And she conceived by the Holy Spirit.*
> > *Hail Mary, full of grace, the Lord is with you.*
> > *Blessed are you among women,*
> > *and blessed is the fruit of your womb, Jesus.*
> > *Holy Mary, Mother of God, pray for us sinners,*
> > *now and at the hour of our death.*

During the second set of three bells, pray:

> *Here am I, the servant of the Lord;*
> *Let it be with me according to your word.*
> > *Hail Mary, full of grace …*

During the third set of three bells, pray:

The Word was made flesh,
And lived among us.
 Hail Mary, full of grace …

During the set of nine bells, pray:

Pour your grace into our hearts, O Lord,
that we who have known the incarnation
 of your Son Jesus Christ,
announced by an angel to the Virgin Mary,
May by his cross and passion
be brought to the glory of his resurrection;
who lives and reigns with you,
in the unity of the Holy Spirit,
one God, now and forever. Amen.

Anima Christi
Soul prayer

This is a traditional prayer that can be repeated during a time of
meditation. You can pause after each phrase, thinking about what
it means for you.

Repeated often enough, it will rest in the memory, and will come to mind at moments through the day or night, when you need to calm yourself and enter God's presence. The repetition of these words can quiet a fretful mind and heart.

Soul of Christ, sanctify me.
Body of Christ, save me.
Blood of Christ, refresh me.
Water from the side of Christ, wash me.
Passion of Christ, strengthen me.
O good Jesus, hear me;
within your wounds hide me;
suffer me not to be separated from you.
From the malicious enemy defend me.
At the hour of my death call me,
and bid me come to you,
that with your saints, I may worship you,
throughout eternity. Amen.

Answer to Prayer
Does God answer prayers?

Supplication is prayer for ourselves, whereas intercession is prayer for others. When we offer supplication and intercession, we want our prayers to be answered.

We naturally look for a Yes answer to our prayer, but sometimes God says No or Not Yet. If nothing seems to happen, we may think that God hasn't heard or won't answer. But recognizing that God always hears and always answers prayer can lead us to deeper considerations. Perhaps we didn't ask for the right thing, or perhaps we asked for something that would be harmful for us. Perhaps we failed to consider the wider consequences of a positive answer to our prayer — consequences that are apparent to God. In these cases, we can be grateful that God doesn't always say Yes.

Sometimes we are so sure that we're not going to get an answer that, when we do receive what we want, we put it down to coincidence or luck rather than God's gift. Why don't we expect a positive answer? Perhaps we don't want to be indebted to God. Perhaps we think we don't deserve to be heard, let alone answered. But Jesus said,

> *Ask, and it will be given you; search, and you will find;*
> *knock, and the door will be opened for you. For everyone*
> *who asks receives, and everyone who searches finds, and*
> *for everyone who knocks, the door will be opened*
> (Matthew 7:7, 8).

In this same passage, Jesus tells us that God overlooks our shortcomings and responds to our prayers because we are children of God.

> *Is there anyone among you who, if your child asks for*
> *bread, will give a stone? Or if the child asks for a fish,*
> *will give a snake? If you then, who are evil, know how to*

give good gifts to your children, how much more will your
Father in heaven give good things to those who ask him
(Matthew 7:9–11).

Sometimes when we pray, we have a preconceived idea of what
the answer will be. But God loves to surprise us. We need to be
open for an unusual answer. When you shake the apple tree,
don't be surprised if the universe gives you oranges! Sometimes,
many years down the road, we may look back and see with surprise that God did indeed answer our prayers.

Prayer suggestions

- Spend a few minutes now to review your life. Look back a
  few days, a few months, a few years.
- See if you can detect God's answers to your prayers, or his
  path for your life, even when you didn't ask. Expect his answer to your prayer.
- Examine something you received. Did it make you happy?
  Was it something you had asked for? Did you put it down to
  coincidence? Could it have been God's answer to prayer?
- Accept God's gifts to you with thanks and joy.

Anxiety
Can we expect God to clothe us like the lilies of the field?

We need food to eat, clothes to keep us warm, shelter over our heads, and money to get these things. Even though we may believe that God will provide for us, we worry about how our needs will be supplied.

The parable of the ravens and the lilies tells us that we are not to worry. We are assured that, when we ask for what we need, God will supply.

> *Consider the ravens: they neither sow nor reap, they have neither storehouse nor barn, and yet God feeds them. Of how much more value are you than the birds!... Consider the lilies, how they grow: they neither toil nor spin; yet I tell you, even Solomon in all his glory was not clothed like one of these. But if God so clothes the grass of the field, which is alive today and tomorrow is thrown into the oven, how much more will he clothe you — you of little faith! And do not keep striving for what you are to eat and what you are to drink, and do not keep worrying. For it is the nations of the world that strive after all these things, and your Father knows that you need them. Instead, strive for his kingdom, and these things will be given to you as well* (Luke 12:24, 27–31).

This is difficult to accept at face value. Yes, we know that God feeds the birds and clothes the flowers and the grass. But what does the parable mean for us? Surely we won't get clothes and food unless we work for them. We have been taught to be practical: "God helps those who help themselves."

The parable begins to make sense when we look at its conclusion: "Strive for his kingdom, and these things will be given to you as well." What is the kingdom? For each of us it means something different because it includes the fulfillment of God's vocation or calling for each of us. When we answer God's calling and say, "Yes, Lord, I will do it," then, through the grace of God, the means are provided.

The raven is called by God to be a raven, and Christ tells us that in fulfilling that life, the raven will be fed. The flowers of the field are created by God to be flowers, and in fulfillment of that creation, each is clothed in its own raiment — daylilies in bright orange, poppies in flaming red, primroses in delicate yellow.

A tree gives glory to God by being a tree. For in being what God means it to be it is obeying him (Thomas Merton, New Seeds of Contemplation).

The parable means, then, that if we try to discern God's vocation and respond to it, we can cease to be anxious. God will not call us to do something and then abandon us. The way may not be easy. It may require daily waiting upon God to supply our needs, but God provides even the faith to wait.

How much easier it would be to depend upon ourselves. How often do we say, "If you want something done right, you have to do it yourself"? By "right" we mean the way we think it should be done. But we see only a small part of our life's tapestry; God sees the whole. It may be years before we can look back and see God's guiding hand. Today we're asked to trust that God is leading us on the way that is in our best interest.

When I can't figure out what is happening in my life, I say, "God, it has always worked out before and I have to trust that all will be well now. If it turns out that I don't get this job, or don't find this friend, or am not healed of this sickness, I have to presume that there is something else for me. God, I believe; help my unbelief."

Prayer suggestions

- ∞ "Lord, I am afraid to rely on you as the ravens and the lilies do. Give me the faith I need."
- ∞ "Lord, I believe that your purpose for me is … (Say out loud what you believe God wants you to do.)"
- ∞ "Lord, I desire to follow your purpose for me."
- ∞ "Lord, I believe that you will provide what I need in order that I may follow my purpose."

Arrow Prayers
Short, sharp prayers

An arrow prayer is a short, sharp request or statement that is intended to speed directly to God. It is an immediate response to a specific situation. An arrow prayer could be a cry for help, as we might call out to a friend or parent if we fall down or land in a crisis. It could be a cry of gratitude or relief, if we receive some wonderful intuition or kindness. An arrow prayer trusts that God is with us in the situation, and hears us right now.

Such quick, little prayers for help can be made with confidence because God is ready to give what we need even before we ask. Our prayer is a confirmation that we believe God will answer.

> *Before they call I will answer, while they are yet speaking I will hear* (Isaiah 65:24).

Arrow prayers of thanks and joy affirm our confidence in God's continual presence and love. God is with us, and we share in the bounty of the Lord.

Arrow prayer suggestions

∽ "I'm scared, Lord. Help me."
∽ "I can't do it without you, Lord. Help me."

∾ "Stay with me, Lord. Be with me, Lord."

∾ "Thank you, Lord."

∾ "How wonderful, O God."

There are other kinds of arrow prayers that are more like throwing a ball than shooting an arrow. They are prayers of response to being in God's presence. For instance, every morning when I begin my work, I say: "Lord, here I am." These words remind me that God is with me and I am listening.

More arrow prayer suggestions

∾ "Speak, Lord, your servant is listening."

∾ "Here I am, Lord, send me."

∾ "Open my ears that I may hear."

∾ "Be it unto me according to your word."

∾ "Your will be done."

Bless and Blessed
Many meanings

The phrase *to bless* means "to praise, to consecrate, to bestow divine favour, or to be happy."

Bless as praise

The Song of the Three is the song sung by Shadrach, Meshach, and Abednego in the midst of the burning fiery furnace where King Nebuchadnezzar had thrown them. The word "blessed" here is used to show how they revered God and held him worthy of praise. The prayer may be found in the Book of Daniel, chapter three, verses fifty-two to fifty-seven.

Blessed are you, O Lord, God of our ancestors,
and to be praised and highly exalted forever.

And blessed is your glorious, holy name,
and to be highly praised and highly exalted forever.

Blessed are you in the temple of your holy glory,
and to be extolled and highly glorified forever.

Blessed are you who look into the depths
  from your throne on the cherubim,
and to be praised and highly exalted forever.

Blessed are you on the throne of your kingdom,
and to be extolled and highly exalted forever.

Blessed are you in the firmament of heaven,
and to be sung and glorified forever.

Bless the Lord, all you works of the Lord;
sing praise to him and highly exalt him forever.

The prayer continues by calling upon all creation to bless — that is, praise — the Lord. It can be found in the Bible in the place indicated above, and also in *The Book of Alternative Services* as Canticles 13, 14, 15, and 16 (pages 82–85) and in *The Book of Common Prayer* as the canticle "Benedicite Omnia Opera" (pages 26–28).

Bless as consecrate

At meals we ask God to consecrate the gifts of food and to strengthen us for service.

Bless, O Lord, this food to our use and us to your service,
for the sake of Jesus Christ our Lord. Amen

Bless as prayer for God's favour upon people

At the end of the Holy Eucharist and other church services, the bishop or priest requests God's favour by pronouncing a blessing on the people in the congregation.

The Lord bless you and keep you;
the Lord make his face to shine upon you,
*   and be gracious to you;*
the Lord lift up his countenance upon you, and give you
peace (Numbers 6:24–26).

Bless as happiness

The Beatitudes were spoken by Christ in what is known as the Sermon on the Mount. They startlingly contradict a secular understanding of happiness and are worth many hours of meditation. Few words can convey such profound comfort and encouragement.

Blessed are the poor in spirit, for theirs is the kingdom of
*   heaven.*
Blessed are those who mourn, for they will be comforted.
Blessed are the meek, for they will inherit the earth.
Blessed are those who hunger and thirst for righteousness,
*   for they will be filled.*
Blessed are the merciful, for they will receive mercy.

Blessed are the pure in heart, for they will see God.
Blessed are the peacemakers, for they will be called
    children of God.
Blessed are those who are persecuted for righteousness'
    sake, for theirs is the kingdom of heaven.
Blessed are you when people revile you and persecute you
    and utter all kinds of evil against you falsely on my
    account. Rejoice and be glad, for your reward is great
    in heaven (Matthew 5:3–12).

Born Anew
New birth every day

Many of us were brought up in our parents' faith, baptized as infants, and taken to church and Sunday school to receive the teachings. By baptism with water and the Holy Spirit we died to the old life and were born again to new life in Christ.

Throughout our lives we experience a deepening awareness and growing understanding of the Spirit that we have already received. Such insight may come suddenly at special moments, or gradually over time. In this way the seed that was planted in us at our baptism grows, flowers, and comes to fruition.

When Nicodemus approached Jesus to learn about his teachings, he came by night. It would not have been expedient for a man in his position to speak with Jesus openly, but he wanted to see for himself and make up his own mind. Nicodemus was already following God's law in the religion of his ancestors, but the Spirit stirred him to find out more about Jesus, whose teaching made him wonder if there might be something more to a relationship with God than simply obeying written laws.

> Nicodemus came to Jesus by night and said to him, "Rabbi, we know that you are a teacher who has come from God; for no one can do these signs that you do apart from the presence of God." Jesus answered him, "Very truly, I tell you, no one can see the kingdom of God without being born from above." Nicodemus said to him, "How can anyone be born after having grown old? Can one enter a second time into the mother's womb and be born?" Jesus answered, "Very truly, I tell you, no one can enter the kingdom of God without being born of water and Spirit. What is born of the flesh is flesh, and what is born of the Spirit is spirit" (John 3:2–6).

We don't know how Nicodemus responded to the teachings of Jesus. It seems likely that he became a disciple, perhaps secretly (John 19:39–42). God showed him alternatives but left him to make up his own mind. This is what God does with us at every turn in our life's journey. We are continually being born again in our spiritual life. If we become sick in body and then are healed, we say that we feel like a new person. If we become sick in spirit, confess our weakness to God, and receive forgiveness, we feel renewed. Each time we reach a new understanding of our relationship with God, it is like a new birth.

You have been born anew, not of perishable but of imperishable seed, through the living and enduring word of God (1 Peter 1:23).

Prayer suggestions

∾ Consider the following Bible verses in meditation:

Create in me a clean heart, O God, and put a new and right spirit within me (Psalm 51:11).

I will give them one heart, and put a new spirit within them (Ezekiel 11:19).

I will give a white stone, and on the white stone is written a new name that no one knows except the one who receives it (Revelation 2:17).

Bread

Meditation while making bread — practising the presence of God

The practice of the presence of God, or praying without ceasing, leads us to hear God's word in surprising ways.

One morning I was meditating while baking bread. Many different ingredients can be added to the basic recipe of water, flour, and yeast. Bread may be leavened or unleavened. A recipe for leavened bread may use yeast, or it may call for baking powder and soda to make it rise. Breads that use yeast will take longer, sometimes even requiring two risings, while those that use baking powder and soda will be faster.

The cycle of the church year is rather like the making of bread. The long season of Trinity, or ordinary time, is like slow yeast bread, while the shorter seasons of Advent and Lent are like quick soda bread, culminating after a few weeks in the festivals of Christmas and Easter.

God's working in our lives has a lot in common with bread making. When we start, the bread is a messy-looking mixture of flour, yeast, water, and a little sugar, salt, and oil. As we stir, it becomes a sticky lump of dough. The kneading of the dough is like God's hands shaping us. We consist of all the right ingredients, but we are an unformed mixture. Then as God works in us, pushing and pulling, folding with quarter turns, we become something living. Just as a person kneading can feel life enter into the dough, can feel the stickiness become elastic and responsive beneath the hands, so God sees the change and development in us. We too become aware of new life within us.

Then comes the waiting time. After the kneading, we leave the dough to rise in a covered bowl in a warm room, protected from draughts until it reaches twice its original size. When we first learn to wait in quiet prayer, we too grow in the warmth and security of God's love, knowing with confidence that God is working in our lives.

Next the dough is punched down. After it has risen a second time, we divide it into loaves, put it into prepared pans, then cover it again and leave it in a warm place. Certainly we too get punched down. Some harsh reality takes us from the warm spot where we were growing so comfortably, and knocks the wind out of us — sickness, loss, unemployment, divorce. Kneaded and broken in pieces, we are left to rise again. Our spiritual life is not dead, though sometimes we wonder if we will ever recover from the blows we have received.

After a time of waiting in the warmth, the broken and divided pieces grow again, and the dough doubles in size. So too, through trials and sorrows, our spiritual life grows again. We find that God is still there. God has used our difficulties to help us mature. Our prayer has reached a different stage. It is stronger because, even though we were beaten down, God did not desert us.

Now the dough is put into the oven where it browns and bakes, so that it can feed us and others. We too, now that we have come through spiritual testing, are ready to get on with life and make our contribution to the world. Through our experiences and difficulties, through our reading and meditation, through our learning from others, we are strengthened and readied to enjoy life and to serve others.

When the baked bread is eaten, we have to bake more. In our spiritual lives we have to replenish the inner supply. Through quiet days and retreats, through prayer and reading, through communion with people of spiritual insight, we are fed and renewed. The cycle continues. As we grow in the Lord, so we are prepared for further spiritual growth by a round of trials and joys, difficulties and happiness, troubles and assistance. God does not ask a greater burden of us than we can bear.

Meditation suggestion

- Choose some solitary activity you enjoy. It can be a very ordinary activity. Think of each separate stage of the activity. Consider how you extend your knowledge and appreciation of this activity into other areas of your life: for example, cooking, cleaning, gardening, walking, driving, building, or repairing.

Called and Chosen

What does it mean to be chosen by God?

You did not choose me but I chose you. And I appointed you to go and bear fruit, fruit that will last, so that the Father will give you whatever you ask him in my name. I am giving you these commands so that you may love one another (John 15:16, 17).

We are called and chosen by God to be Christ's heirs. St. Paul tells us that we were chosen in Christ, even before the world was made.

*[God] chose us in Christ before the foundation of the
world to be holy and blameless before him in love. He
destined us for adoption as his children through Jesus
Christ (Ephesians 1:4, 5).*

So then, we are called and chosen by God to love one another as
Christ loves us. God chose us, not for any particular merits of
our own. In fact, God takes delight in calling ordinary people.

*Consider your own call, brothers and sisters: not many
of you were wise by human standards, not many were
powerful, not many were of noble birth. But God chose
what is foolish in the world to shame the wise; God
chose what is weak in the world to shame the strong
(1 Corinthians 1:26, 27).*

That we have been called and chosen to be heirs of Christ to his
kingdom doesn't mean that we have nothing to do. We are called
to love — to love God and our neighbour. God also asks us to
pray and meditate upon our calling.

*I pray that the God of our Lord Jesus Christ, the Father
of glory, may give you a spirit of wisdom and revelation
as you come to know him, so that with the eyes of your
heart enlightened, you may know what is the hope to
which he has called you, what are the riches of his glorious inheritance among the saints, and what is the im-
measurable greatness of his power for us who believe
(Ephesians 1:17–19).*

At first glance it is amazing that God should acknowledge us at all, considering the vastness of creation. So with great wonder and awe and thanksgiving, we meditate upon God's call to us:

> *When I look at your heavens,*
> *the work of your fingers,*
> *the moon and the stars that you have established;*
> *what are human beings that you*
> *are mindful of them,*
> *mortals that you care for them?*
> (Psalm 8:3, 4).

Not only does he acknowledge us, he calls us to be his followers, even his friends. Jesus says,

> *I have called you friends, because I have made known to*
> *you everything thta I have heard from my Father*
> (John 15:15).

In response, we are moved to love, pray, and work with God to bring about the kingdom on earth.

Prayer and action suggestions

- Thank God that he has called you and chosen you. Can you remember times when you heard God's call?
- Consider what it means to you to be called and chosen by God.
- What will you do to respond to God's calling?

Christ in Me

Acknowledging the presence of Christ in each other

When I visited the Anglican convent of St. John the Divine in the 1960s, I noticed that the nuns had a quaint custom of curtsying whenever they encountered one another. Some months later, I discovered that there was more to this act than an old-fashioned practice. The nuns curtsied to one another in order to reverence the Christ in each person. Now it follows that, if we acknowledge the presence of Christ in another person, we must also recognize the Christ abiding in ourselves. We must therefore respect ourselves as temples of Christ and the Holy Spirit.

> *Do you not know that your body is a temple of the Holy Spirit within you, which you have from God, and that you are not your own? For you were bought with a price; therefore glorify God in your body* (1 Corinthians 6:19, 20).

> *I have been crucified with Christ; and it is no longer I who live, but it is Christ who lives in me* (Galatians 2:19, 20).

Knowing that Christ is within us, we must endeavour not to restrict his actions. We need to practise setting him free, so that he can live and act and pray in his fullness through us. This isn't easy. We may try to live and act as Christ wants us to, but our human frailty often hinders Christ from acting freely in us. Here are some helps for freeing the Christ within.

Meditation suggestions

- ∾ In order to allow him the freedom to work as if you and he were one person, try picturing yourself standing behind Christ. Let him be front and centre stage. You are the supporting actor; Christ is the lead.
- ∾ Think of yourself as one of a number of people who are under Christ's direction, like a group of dancers or a choir of singers. Your heart, mind, and spirit provide the means of expression, but Christ is the choreographer, the conductor.
- ∾ Consider saints of our time who learned to let Christ work through them, people like Mother Teresa, Jean Vanier, Corrie ten Boon. Let them inspire you to allow Christ to work freely through you.

Cleansing the Spiritual Water

How to keep the living water pure

Clear flowing water is an apt image of the spirit. In particular I like to picture the river of water flowing from God's throne, as described by St. John in the Book of Revelation.

The water that is our spiritual essence arises in Christ. Sometimes the events of life can muddy or clog the flow. The waters of our spirit may become murky with worries, overwork, addictions, even good times and pleasures. Then we need to return in prayer to the source that is Christ to supply us with clean clear water. Our newly cleansed water will sparkle in the sunlight, reflecting the radiance that comes from God and shines through us to others.

Our spiritual stream or well needs to be constantly replenished with rain from God. Whether God's rain is gentle and steady like greening spring showers or sudden and heavy like mid-summer storms, it renews our spirit with fresh insights and ideas. When through prayer and meditation we let the rain of God replenish our spiritual streams, we feel alive and blessed.

Spiritual exercises

- Think of your spiritual being as water. Do you see yourself as a stream, a spring, a well, or an oasis?

∽ See the pure river of God flowing into your spiritual being. Thank God for this life-giving water. Do you see any debris in your own stream or well? Name the debris.

∽ What can you do to clean out the debris? Name one action you can do to cleanse your spiritual water. Commit to that act. For example, suppose that the debris is from overwork or a quarrel. Take a half-hour from your overwork and spend it in meditation or spiritual reading. Forgive the person you have quarrelled with, and receive the person's forgiveness.

∽ Are you feeling spiritually empty? Take the time to be replenished by God's rain. Perhaps take an hour or a day to be alone with God. Ask God to fill you with the water of life.

∽ When you are filled with God's clear water and your spiritual spring is clean, give freely of the water of life to others. Is there someone you know in need of spiritual drink? Name that person. Commit to helping that person find spiritual refreshment.

Compline
Prayer at the end of the day

Compline is a service to be said at the end of the day. Its root word is *complete*. Saying Compline completes the day. The service contains requests and assurances that we will be kept from harm through the night. It prepares us for repose.

I will both lie down and sleep in peace;
for you alone, O Lord,
make me lie down in safety (Psalm 4:8).

For he will command his angels to guard you in all your
ways (Psalm 91:11).

Compline can be said in a group, as a fine way to end an evening meeting, or it can be read by an individual. It is very reassuring if you live alone. Even if you do not say the whole service, you can use parts of it as prayer before you go to sleep. Some of these prayers can be found under "Home Prayers" on page 692 of *The Book of Alternative Services* of the Anglican Church of Canada.

In monastic communities, where the traditional services — the seven hours — are said, Compline is the last office of the day and leads into the Greater Silence. This time of silence lasts for about twelve hours, from Compline till Terce the following morning. Only necessary words are spoken.

A great peace descends on the monastery after Compline. Each member of the community holds Christ close in the heart, knowing that to speak unnecessarily can break this peace for themselves and others.

You, O Lord, are in the midst of us, and we are called by
your name; do not forsake us (Jeremiah 14:9).

Guard me as the apple of your eye;
hide me in the shadow of your wings (Psalm 17:8).

- ∾ Say one of the psalms designated for Compline — Psalm 4, 91, or 134.
- ∾ Just before you sleep, thank God for guiding you through your day, and ask for safety through the night.
- ∾ Join yourself in imagination with the peaceful silence of a monastery. Rest in this silence and sleep in trust.

Contrition
Crushed in spirit but not broken

When I looked up *contrition* in the *Concise Oxford Dictionary*, I was surprised to find that it means "crushed in spirit." I had thought that the word meant "to be very sorry," and I had always felt consoled by Psalm 51:17.

> *The sacrifice acceptable to God is a broken spirit;*
> *a broken and contrite heart, O God, you will not despise.*

Now, I am not so sure. Would God really be glad if my heart were broken and crushed? Does God really want my spirit to be troubled? Certainly God is not demanding that we suffer sorrow or pain. Instead, God is reaching out to us when our hearts have been crushed and our spirits have been disturbed, and God is lovingly accepting our pain as a sacrifice.

*A bruised reed he will not break, and a dimly burning
wick he will not quench* (Isaiah 42:3).

*Rend your hearts and not your clothing. Return to the
Lord, your God, for he is gracious and merciful, slow to
anger, and abounding in steadfast love, and relents from
punishing* (Joel 2:13).

Many trials and sorrows and disappointments may break our
hearts. What must it be like when your home is destroyed and
your family killed, and you leave everything behind as a refu-
gee? The sin that inflicted these horrors can crush the hearts of
the sinners too. What must it be like to know that you are re-
sponsible for causing pain and suffering? God can restore spiritual
health to both the perpetrators and the victims — and there is a
little of both in all of us.

As pain in the body alerts us to a physical ailment and a
healing solution, so contrition wakes us up to a spiritual problem and leads us to confession with its resulting forgiveness. It is
this process that makes our spirits whole and returns us to a
right relationship with God and ourselves.

Prayer suggestions

- ∾ Take a quiet moment with God. Does your heart feel crushed
  or your spirit feel disturbed? Look to find the cause.
- ∾ If there is something in your life that temporarily separates
  you from God, tell God you are sorry and ask forgiveness.
- ∾ Thank God for forgiveness. Thank God for making you whole
  again.

Covenant

An agreement between you and God

A covenant is an agreement or a bargain. In the Old Testament it is a contract between God and the Israelites. Moses tells the Israelites,

> You stand assembled today … to enter into the covenant
> of the Lord your God, sworn by an oath, which the Lord
> your God is making with you today; in order that he may
> establish you today as his people, and that he may be your
> God, as he promised you (Deuteronomy 29:10, 12, 13).

Our spiritual growth does not cease once a covenant has been made between us and God. Instead, we go on seeking God ever more deeply, and discover eventually that God is within us and we are within God.

> That they would search for God and perhaps grope for
> him and find him — though indeed he is not far from each
> one of us. For "In him we live and move and have our
> being" (Acts 17:27, 28).

In his poem, "The Hound of Heaven," Francis Thompson assures us that, no matter what happens, God will not let us go.

> I fled Him, down the nights and down the days;
> I fled Him, down the arches of the years;
> I fled Him, down the labyrinthine ways

Of my own mind, and in the mist of tears
I hid from Him, and under running laughter.
Up vistaed hopes I sped;
And shot, precipitated,
Adown Titanic glooms of chasmed fears,
From those strong Feet that followed, followed after.
But with unhurrying chase ...

Prayer suggestions

∞ Lord, I know that you have made a covenant with me, that I am yours and you are my God.

∞ Lord, sometimes I forget that we have an agreement that you will live in me and I in you. I search for you elsewhere.

∞ Lord, I now renew my remembrance of our covenant and take hold of the promise of eternal inheritance.

Daily Prayer
Making a prayer schedule

Your choice of pattern for daily prayer will depend on the time available to you, your religious denomination, where you are on the spiritual path. You may already have a prayer pattern set out for yourself.

But if you are just beginning to look for one, I would suggest that you start small, rather than commit to too much and become discouraged. You can always build more into it later.

Whatever form your prayer may take, your relationship with God will develop as you pray, just as your relationship with a friend grows as you talk with each other.

∞ Daily prayer can be a short word with God when you first get up in the morning. "Lord, I give myself to you this day."

∞ After the alarm goes off and before you get out of bed, focus quietly on God and offer your day to God. Ask God to guide you and keep you safe.

∞ Speak to God before you go to sleep. You could go through ACTS: Adoration, Confession, Thanksgiving, and Supplication.

∞ Say the Lord's Prayer, or Psalm 23.

∞ If you wish to have a more structured prayer time, there are many daily prayer books or leaflets available.

The Revised Common Lectionary supplies psalm and Bible readings for each day of the year, as well as prayers for the season and special occasions. It also has an outline for morning and evening prayer.

Booklets such as *Forward Day by Day* and *The Upper Room* give daily devotions with Bible readings, a reflection, and prayer.

The *Breviary*, the *Monastic Diurnal*, and the Anglican Franciscan office book, *Celebrating Common Prayer,* give daily offices recited in religious orders.

Monastic orders, both Anglican and Roman Catholic, have associates and oblates who follow a Rule of Life that includes prayers and someone to guide you in spiritual growth.

Many web pages on the Internet are devoted to prayer; some give a daily service. Many offer opportunities to make or receive intercessory prayer.

Darkness and Light
Darkness is no different from light with God

Although many of us are frightened by the dark, the Bible often uses darkness as an image of protection, or assures us that the dark is as light as the day if we are with God.

> *He made darkness his covering around him,*
> *his canopy thick clouds dark with water. ...*
> *It is you who light my lamp;*
> *the Lord, my God,*
> *lights up my darkness*
> (Psalm 18:11, 28).

> *If I say, "Surely the darkness shall cover me,*
> *and the light around me become night,"*
> *even the darkness is not dark to you;*
> *the night is as bright as the day:*
> *for darkness is as light to you*
> (Psalm 139:11, 12).

When God created the heavens and the erath, the earth
was a formless void and darkness covered the face of the
deep, while a wind from God swept over the face of the
waters. Then God said, "Let there be light" (Genesis 1:1–3).

The Easter Vigil is a celebration of the coming of light from dark-ness. From Good Friday until Holy Saturday no candles are lit in the church. Christ, the Light of the world, has died, and we show this symbolically by leaving the candles unlit. On the Eve of Easter, the church has a ritual of lighting the new fire. This fire represents Christ's rising from the tomb on the third day after his crucifixion. New light and hope shine forth. From the fire, the paschal candle is lit and carried down the main body of the church. The deacon or priest who carries it makes three stops, raises the candle aloft and sings, "The Light of Christ." The con-gregation responds by singing the words, "Thanks be to God." Each person lights a candle from the new flame, the darkness is banished, and the whole church is filled with light. We, too, are filled with joy as the light shines around and in us, giving reas-surance of Christ's resurrection and our salvation.

Creativity — like human life itself — begins in darkness.
We need to acknowledge this.... It is true that insights
may come to us in flashes.... It is also true that such
bright ideas are preceded by a gestation period that is
interior, murky, and completely necessary" (Julia
Cameron, The Artist's Way).

Our thoughts too are lit by the spark of the Spirit and often smoul-der for a long time before they are fanned into flames. Out of random thoughts and ideas comes the fire of new creation in the form of words or art or healing.

Fire can destroy, but destruction of the old can lead to creation of the new. Destruction of forests by fire allows new growth, because seeds that have waited for many years burst their skins in the heat, put down roots into the soil, and send shoots into the air.

Prayer suggestions

- ∽ Ask God to be with you and protect you in the dark.
- ∽ Ask God to light the spark of new fire, and to be your light in the dark.
- ∽ Ask God to light your way out of the dark and into new life.
- ∽ Thank God for being the light and fire of new life and growth.

Delight
Take pleasure in being in God's presence

Take delight in the Lord,
and he will give you the desires of your heart (Psalm 37:4).

The quality of life is in proportion, always, to the capacity
for delight. The capacity of delight is the gift of paying
attention (Julia Cameron, The Artist's Way*).*

Psalm 37 tells us that, if we delight in the Lord, he will give us our heart's desire. As our delight in God increases, we become more aware of God's gifts to us. We find ourselves taking pleasure in a baby's smile, a friend's voice, a rainstorm, a daisy flowering by the roadside. The more we delight in God and realize what good things we do have, the greater our capacity for appreciating and receiving God's gifts and passing them on to others.

Jesus said, "To those who have, more will be given, and they will have an abundance" (Matthew 13:12).

As our delight in God and God's creation grows, we become happier and more contented. Other people see this and are naturally drawn toward us. We may find that they spontaneously do things for us — send a greeting card or bring us a flower from their garden, telephone or spend time with us, invite us to accompany or visit them, encourage our plans and projects and, in times of need, stay by our side. People find it easier to do things for people who are contented and happy.

Mother Teresa started a community that served the poor and dying in the name of Christ. Her delight in the Lord led her to give herself completely to God and to the poorest of the poor. In doing the most difficult work, she drew many people to her. As other communities diminished and suffered from lack of vocations, women from all around the world flocked to her community. As their love of neighbour increased, so did their capacity for delight in the Lord.

I ask you to do one thing: do not tire of giving, but do not give your leftovers. Give until it hurts, until you feel the pain (Mother Teresa).

*Mother Teresa is very clear in her goals: to love and serve
the poor, seeing Jesus in them. She has always left the
ways and means to do this in God's hands (José Luis
Gonzalez-Balado,* Mother Teresa: In My Own Words*).*

Prayer suggestions

- ⚭ "O Lord, I take delight in you. As I delight in you, I become
  more aware of the wonder of all your creation. I take pleasure, not only in you, O Lord, but also in the works of your
  hands."
- ⚭ "I thank you for the feeling of joy this gives to me. I thank
  you for others who share their gifts with me."
- ⚭ "I want to share my delight in you, O Lord, with others."
- ⚭ Name one way you can share your joy of him with others.
  Volunteer in an adult literacy group. Help with a Sunday
  school class. Think of the best way you could share your
  delight in the Lord with others.
- ⚭ Commit to an action to make this happen.

Distractions

How to deal with distractions in prayer

Distracting thoughts that come during prayer and meditation are like wayward children demanding attention. If we struggle against them, they will cling to us and cause more anxiety because, in a way, they belong to us. A simple acknowledgement of them reassures the mind that we don't underestimate their importance and won't forget them. Then we can gently let them go for the time being and continue our spiritual practice.

Why do things we haven't thought of for days come to distract us as soon as we have time to meditate? When we stop being busy, the mind has a chance to remember things. Instead of occupying itself with prayer as we had planned, it reminds us of hurts and pleasures and needs and responsibilities. In fact, God may be prompting us to deal with these things. But if we start planning the details of future action there and then, we will be thoroughly distracted from meditation.

Even people such as Brother Lawrence and Thomas Merton, who devoted most of their lives to spiritual practice, were troubled by distractions. This is a comfort for all on the path of prayer, both the experienced and the beginner.

> No matter how distracted you may be, pray by peaceful,
> even perhaps inarticulate, efforts to centre your heart
> upon God, who is present to you in spite of all that may
> be going through your mind. His presence does not depend
> on your thoughts of him. He is unfailingly there; if he

were not, you could not even exist. *The memory of his unfailing presence is the surest anchor for our minds and hearts in the storm of distraction and temptation by which we must be purified* (Thomas Merton, New Seeds of Contemplation).

I worshipped him the oftenest that I could, keeping my mind in his holy presence, and recalling it as often as I found it wandered from him. I found no small pain in this exercise, and yet I continued it, notwithstanding all the difficulties that occurred, without troubling or disquieting myself when my mind had wandered involuntarily (Brother Lawrence, The Practice of the Presence of God).

Suggestion

ꙮ During your meditation have a notebook or piece of paper at hand. Write the distractions down as they arise. They could be things to do today, things you need from the store, someone you want to telephone. They could be memories of pain or trouble, happiness or good fortune. When you write them down, they lose their power to distract because you know that they will not be forgotten.

Doubt

Faith is shown in action, not feeling

Without doubt we would simply believe everything we are told by the media, by business and government leaders, by the people around us. Doubt is a very healthy frame of mind. Modern science, which has brought us medical advances and many other helps and comforts, depends on the constructive use of doubt. When scientists doubt what the old authorities have always said, they may be on the verge of a new discovery.

After Jesus' resurrection several of his disciples, who had seen the master they thought was dead, told their experience to Thomas. He replied, "Unless I see the mark of the nails in his hands, and put my finger in the mark of the nails and my hand in his side, I will not believe." When he met the master, Jesus invited him, "Put your finger here and see my hands. Reach out your hand and put it in my side. Do not doubt but believe" (see John 20:24–29).

Jesus seems to have accepted that Thomas was behaving like a good scientist! When Jesus said, "Blessed are those who have not seen and yet have come to believe," he was not criticizing Thomas. More likely, he was accepting the perhaps simpler faith of those who did not feel the need of the kind of proof that convinced Thomas.

It helps us to know that Jesus too had his moment of doubt. In all things he was tested as we are, and he understands our doubt and feelings of abandonment.

Jesus went with them to a place called Gethsemane; and he said to his disciples, "Sit here while I go over there and pray" … "I am deeply grieved, even to death; remain here, and stay awake with me." Then he came to the disciples and found them sleeping; and he said to Peter, "So, could you not stay awake with me one hour?" (Matthew 26:36, 38, 40).

For we do not have a high priest who is unable to sympathize with our weaknesses, but we have one who in every respect has been tested as we are, yet without sin. Let us therefore approach the throne of grace with boldness, so that we may receive mercy and find grace to help in time of need (Hebrews 4:15, 16).

As Christ asked his disciples to stay and watch with him, so, in our times of doubt, we can ask others to pray for us. In our turn, we can support others in their times of struggle and weakness.

Prayer suggestions

- "Jesus, you experienced feelings of abandonment and doubt. I ask you to support and strengthen me in my doubt, that I might come through my time of trial with greater faith."
- "Jesus, you felt the need for someone to be present with you in your time of distress. Be present with me now."
- "Jesus, you gave others your support, even in your time of greatest agony. Give me the strength and courage to support others, even though I am in turmoil."

Doxology
Hymn of praise

According to the *Concise Oxford Dictionary*, a doxology is a "liturgical formula of praise to God." It occurs in many forms, but almost always it offers praise to God the Holy Trinity: Father, Son, and Holy Spirit. It is often added to the end of a psalm, canticle, or hymn and is a suitable ending for our own prayers or meditations.

The traditional form used in *The Book of Common Prayer* is

Glory be to the Father, and to the Son, and to the Holy Ghost; As it was in the beginning, is now, and ever shall be, world without end. Amen.

In contemporary liturgies, such as those found in *The Book of Alternative Services*, it reads:

Glory to the Father, and to the Son, and to the Holy Spirit: as it was in the beginning, is now, and will be forever. Amen.

The doxology can include other equally biblical and less gender-specific names of God.

Glory and praise to the Creator, to the Redeemer, and to the Sanctifier, now and always. Amen.

Here it is in various forms in the last verses of hymns:

Praise God from whom all blessings flow;
Praise him, all creatures here below;
Praise him above, you heavenly host;
Praise Father, Son and Holy Ghost
(Thomas Ken, 1637–1710).

To Father, Son, and Holy Ghost,
The God whom we adore,
Be glory, as it was, is now,
And shall be evermore
(Tate and Brady, 1696).

Laud and honour to the Father,
Laud and honour to the Son,
Laud and honour to the Spirit,
Ever three and ever one,
One in might, and one in glory,
While unending ages run
(from seventh- or eighth-century Latin, translated by
John Mason Neale).

Early

Praying to God early in the morning

O God, you are my God, I seek you (Psalm 63:1).

Getting up early in the morning for prayers is routine in monastic orders and gives a very powerful beginning to the day. The corporate nature of the first prayers of the day in the chapel of a monastery or convent is almost tangible and reminds us of the unceasing prayers of the saints.

When we say our morning prayers or have a time of meditation alone after experiencing the corporate prayer of a monastic community, we realize that we join with all the voices of praise around the world. There is always somebody somewhere praying to God. If we don't feel strong in the power of prayer on a given day, we can unite our prayer and praise with those of others, so that we may be upheld by their strength.

As day becomes night in our part of the world, somewhere else night becomes day and the prayer continues. Prayer is a continual vigil around the clock as one person after another takes up the work.

Prayer suggestions

∾ Seek the Lord early and eagerly. When you wake up in the morning, dedicate your day to God.

∾ Join your voice and heart with others. Know that your prayer and praise will be carried to God in the strength of others who are praying, even on days when you are distracted.

Fallow Ground
Leaving your spiritual field fallow

The meaning of the word *fallow*, according to the *Concise Oxford Dictionary*, is "ground ploughed and harrowed but left uncropped for a year; uncultivated land."

A farmer rotates crops from one field to another to leave a field fallow or uncultivated for a time, so that the soil may be renewed. With the continuous growing of crops, nutrients in the ground are used up, and in time the crops will become poor and yield little.

Sometimes our spiritual lives seem to be stuck. We go along in a routine, but we feel that nothing is happening. Our prayer life seems dry and barren. We need time for rest and renewal. Our spiritual field needs to lie fallow.

These fallow times affect our working life too. Sometimes we are unable to do anything creative. Often this happens because we have neglected "down" time — reading, walking, resting, and looking. The nutrients that renew our work are depleted and need to be replenished.

The farmer can't continually get a good harvest without putting nutrients into the soil and allowing it to gain back its strength. So it is with prayer. We need to allow our prayer life to be renewed. We need time simply to rest in God, to be quiet with God, and to receive the nourishment and strength we need.

Prayer suggestions

∞ Read a preparatory passage before you come to your prayer time, and then just kneel or sit in God's presence and say,

"I'm here, Lord, in your presence. I wait for you to reveal yourself to me. I rest and recuperate in your presence. In your name, I accept this fallow prayer time."

∞ After you have said this, allow yourself to sit and wait quietly in his presence. Then say,

"My field lies fallow waiting to be nourished for the crop ahead. It is hard to wait. Hold me in your hand. Help me to wait quietly, to be still and know that you are God."

Fasting
A means to an end, not an end in itself

Many religions practise fasting. In Christianity, Lent is observed as a fast, especially Ash Wednesday and Good Friday. Traditionally, Friday has also been a day of fasting or abstaining from meat. It is very beneficial to fast occasionally.

Fasting gives us an opportunity to stop being consumers for a while, to let our bodies recuperate from the daily chore of processing food. Giving our digestive organs a holiday has the effect of relaxing our body and freeing our thoughts and feelings. This may in turn give us more mental and emotional energy. We may want to spend this energy in some constructive way, opening ourselves to God in prayer or giving ourselves to others in service.

And so, fasting has implications for our spiritual health as well as our physical fitness. Most of us can choose to fast. But in many parts of the world, people are forced to fast because they have insufficient food. Fasting can help us to become more aware of those who are in greater need than ourselves, and can move us to compassion and action.

Fasting can help to remind us of those closer to home who cannot affort to feed themselves or their children. Then we might be moved to give something to a food bank or to help in a food kitchen. Fasting can also remind us of those who have no joy in their lives. Then we might decide to visit an elderly person, take someone on an outing, join a volunteer group to help others, or pick up the phone and talk to a friend.

Choosing to fast is part of our own personal discipline. The merits derive not from being especially pious, but from letting God recharge our physical and spiritual energies, so that we can increase our influence for good in the world around us.

> Whenever you fast, do not look dismal, like the hypo-crites, for they disfigure their faces so as to show others that they are fasting. Truly I tell you, they have received their reward. But when you fast, put oil on your head and wash your face, so that your fasting may be seen not by others but by your Father who is in secret; and your Father who sees in secret will reward you (Matthew 6:16–18).

Prayer suggestions

- Lord, when I fast, help me to keep it secret. Help me to re-member that the reason for fasting is to get closer to you. Let my fasting be a means of remembering the needs of others.
- Think of one action you can do to help others in need, and commit to it.

Give an item to the food bank.
Pray for someone who is poor.
Volunteer to cook at a local soup kitchen.
Pick up the phone and call someone who may be lonely.

Forgiveness
Forgiveness and healing

St. Mark tells the story of the paralyzed person who was brought to Jesus to be healed.

> *When Jesus saw their faith, he said to the paralytic, "Son, your sins are forgiven"* (Mark 2:5).

The friends of the paralyzed man brought him to Jesus because they wanted to help him. Perhaps they had tried everything and nothing worked. When they arrived at the house where Jesus was, they couldn't get inside because of the crowd. They couldn't even see Jesus, let alone get close enough to make their request. So they climbed up onto the roof, opened a space, and lowered their friend down to Jesus.

When Jesus saw how strong was their determination, he said to the man on the stretcher, "Your sins are forgiven." Released from his burden, the man could walk again. The friends must have been happy, their faith in God must have been renewed, and the bond of friendship among them must have been strengthened.

Not all paralysis is physical; emotional paralysis can be just as real. Sometimes we are so paralyzed by fear, sickness, lack of love, smothering love, poverty, or even riches that we do not know how to go on. If we are wounded in spirit, we are hampered in our work and play. The longer the wound continues to fester, the more paralyzed we become and the more difficult the wound is to ignore. But when we are treated by forgiveness, the process of healing can begin and we can function again. The impediment in our life has been removed.

Forgiveness involves confessing to God and accepting forgiveness. Confession can take place privately in our own hearts or through an intermediary, such as a priest or counsellor. It is difficult to confess to a minister, but it is even harder to confess to, and ask forgiveness from, the one who was wronged. Yet this is a healing step.

The offended person may also need our forgiveness, for often there has been fault on both sides. We too may need our own forgiveness. We are only human and will necessarily fall short at times. When this happens, we need to acknowledge our humanness and accept our shortcomings. We can give thanks for the learning and resolve to continue to grow in Christ.

In getting to the point of realizing our need to forgive and be forgiven, it can be helpful to have the support of friends, like those of the paralyzed man who took so much trouble on his behalf. When we are happy and busy and enjoying life, we may take friends and family for granted. But when something happens to make us unable to carry on, we become dependent upon others to support us and help us to keep going.

We are members of the body of Christ, each with different gifts of the Spirit, each one a part of the whole body. We are not all the same, but we are all seeking God in our lives.

If the whole body were an eye, where would the hearing be? If the whole body were hearing, where would the sense of smell be? ... Now you are the body of Christ and individually members of it (1 Corinthians 12:17, 27).

God sends us friends when we are paralyzed, and their support may bring us to forgiveness.

Suggested actions

- ∾ Join a group of people with the same interests as you: for example, quilting, singing, or reading. Spiritual support can come from such groups as well as specifically religious ones.
- ∾ If some past deed weighs on you, confess your sense of failing to God, either in your own private prayers or to a priest or some trusted friend.
- ∾ Go to the person wronged and say that you are sorry for what you did and ask for forgiveness.
- ∾ If the situation allows it, tell the person that you were hurt too. If your forgiveness is sought, give it gladly; if not, let it go. You can still give your forgiveness in a silent prayer and a squeeze of the hand or a hug.

Francis of Assisi
Enjoying the will of God

Francis of Assisi (1181–1226) is one of the church's most beloved saints. A rich man, he felt called to imitate Christ's example of total obedience to God. Just as Christ left the throne of heaven to be born on earth and live the life of an ordinary human being,

Francis gave up all his riches to live as one of the poor. Just as Christ lived and worked among the outcast of society, so did Francis.

This prayer, "Make me an Instrument of your Peace," expresses his devotion to doing the will of God. We can use it to remind ourselves of God's will for us:

Lord, make me an instrument of your peace.
Where there is hatred, let me sow love,
  Where there is injury, pardon,
  Where there is doubt, faith,
  Where there is despair, hope,
  Where there is darkness, light;
  Where there is sadness, joy.
O, divine Master, grant that I may not so much seek
  To be consoled, as to console;
  To be understood, as to understand,
  To be loved, as to love.
For it is in giving that we receive;
  It is in pardoning that we are pardoned;
  It is in dying that we are born to eternal life. Amen.

For Francis, serving God offered not only pain and suffering but also deep joy. Freed from the distractions that wealth and power can often bring, he took pleasure in the beauty of the natural world around him. The sun was like a brother to him, the water like a sister. Even the death of the body — an inevitable fact of natural life — was like a sister as well. Here is his famous hymn, often called "The Canticle of Brother Sun":

Most High, all-powerful, good Lord,
   to you be praise, glory, honour and all blessing.

Only to you, Most High, do they belong,
   and no one is worthy to call upon your name.

May you be praised, my Lord, with all your creatures,
   especially brother sun,
   through whom you lighten the day for us.

He is beautiful and radiant with great splendour;
   he signifies you, O Most High.

Be praised, my Lord, for sister moon and the stars;
   clear and precious and lovely, they are formed in
   heaven.

Be praised, my Lord, for brother wind
   and by air and clouds, clear skies and all weathers,
   by which you give sustenance to your creatures.

Be praised, my Lord, for sister water,
   who is very useful and humble and precious and pure.

Be praised, my Lord, for brother fire,
   by whom the night is illumined for us:
   he is beautiful and cheerful, full of power and strength.

Be praised, my Lord, for sister, our mother earth,
   who sustains and governs us

and produces diverse fruits
and coloured flowers and grass.

Be praised, my Lord,
by all those who forgive for love of you
and who bear weakness and tribulation.

Blessed are those who bear them in peace:
for you, Most High, they will be crowned.

Be praised, my Lord, for our sister, the death of the body,
from which no one living is able to flee;
woe to those who are dying in mortal sin.

Blessed are those who are found doing your most holy will,
for the second death will do them no harm.

Praise and bless my lord and give him thanks
and serve him with great humility.

Freedom
God cannot be put in a box

God comes in the space and time and emotions we are in now.
God is not limited to a box of our own making, a box fashioned

by our ideas of what religion should look like. God is with us whether we take part in organized religion or not. We may find God in a church service, in the company of friends, or while walking along a country road.

> The world of Celtic spirituality is completely at home with the rhythm and wisdom of the senses. When you read Celtic nature poetry, you see that all the senses are alerted: You hear the sound of the winds, you taste the fruits, and above all you get a wonderful sense of how nature touches human presence. ... In Celtic spirituality, we find a new bridge between the visible and the invisible (John O'Donohue, Anam Cara: A Book of Celtic Wisdom).

Some find God outside the church. They see God within themselves and around them. At all times in our lives we must be true to the way God has set for us. This way may not be the same tomorrow as it is today. It may not be the same today as it was ten years ago. The adventure is in the way, not in the arrival. If we are travelling the way that God has set before us, there can be no guilt. Guilt comes from others' messages to us: "You should do this, you should do that."

> For you did not receive a spirit of slavery to fall back into fear, but you have received a spirit of adoption. When we cry, "Abba! Father!" it is that very Spirit bearing witness with our spirit that we are children of God (Romans 8:15, 16).

> For freedom Christ has set us free. Stand firm, therefore, and do not submit again to a yoke of slavery (Galatians 5:1).

Prayer suggestions

- Each morning, review your commitment to the way God has set for you.

  "Today I will follow where you lead, Lord. Today I will walk with you along this path."

- Offer a prayer of thanksgiving.

  "Thank you, Lord, for the freedom to worship you.
  Thank you, Lord, for your revelation to me
  through the Bible,
  through the church,
  through nature,
  through friends and family."

- Offer a prayer of praise.

  "Lord, I praise you in all the ways you show yourself to me.
  Lord, help me to see you in all parts of life.
  Lord, help me to manifest you to others in my actions to
      them."

Gifts of God
Using the gifts God gives us

Like good stewards of the manifold grace of God, serve one another with whatever gift each of you has received (1 Peter 4:10).

God has given each one of us gifts for our own fulfillment and for the good of all. When we use our gifts, we give glory to God.

There are varieties of gifts, but the same Spirit; and there are varieties of services, but the same Lord; and there are varieties of activities, but it is the same God who activates all of them in everyone (1 Corinthians 12:4–6).

St. Paul names the gifts of the Spirit several times in his letters (1 Corinthians 12–13; Galatians 5:22; Romans 12:6–8). Most people would immediately add artistic talent or intellectual capacity. But there are many other abilities that need to be recognized — parenting children, caring for the sick, showing kindness to the hurt, being committed to a career, working as a volunteer. There must be as many gifts as there are people in the world.

In his parable of the talents, Jesus tells us that, if we try to preserve and hoard our gifts out of fear, we may lose them. But if we develop and employ our gifts, we may acquire even more.

> Then the one who had received the one talent also came forward, saying, "Master, I knew that you were a harsh man, reaping where you did not sow, and gathering where you did not scatter seed; so I was afraid, and I went and hid your talent in the ground. Here you have what is yours." But his master replied, "You wicked and lazy slave! You knew, did you, that I reap where I did not sow, and gather where I did not scatter? Then you ought to have invested my money with the bankers, and on my return I would have received what was my own with interest. So take the talent from him, and give it to the one with the ten talents. For to all those who have, more will be given, and they will have an abundance; but from those who have nothing, even what they have will be taken away" (Matthew 25:24–29).

We may ask, What about those who have missed the opportunity to develop their gifts, perhaps through confusion or poverty or sickness, through misfortune or misguidance? Surely Jesus would not criticize or condemn people in such circumstances. In Christ's parable of the labourers (Matthew 20:1–16) he makes it clear that, no matter when in life we come to the realization of our gifts and begin to use them, our reward will be the same.

Whatever our past disappointments or present hindrances, we have a mission, both to ourselves and to others, to let our gifts shine as a light in the world. It is never too late!

> *You are the light of the world. A city built on a hill cannot be hid. No one after lighting a lamp puts it under the bushel basket, but on the lampstand, and it gives light to all in the house. In the same way, let your light shine before others, so that they may see your good works and give glory to your Father in heaven* (Matthew 5:14–16).

Prayer suggestions

∽ Name the gifts God has given you. Ask God to help you to share them with others. Ask God to help you have faith that, in sharing your gifts with others, your gifts will not lessen but increase.

∽ Choose one gift from your list. State the way you will use this gift for others. Mark your calendar for one month, and check whether the gift has been depleted or increased by your using it.

∽ Perhaps you are just starting out in life and you are uncertain what gifts you have or how to use them. Spend time in prayer with God. Research your options. Again, spend time in prayer.

∽ Perhaps you are approaching retirement and you want to keep active and interested in life. Spend time in prayer with God. Research your options. Again, spend time in prayer.

Greatest in the Kingdom
Follow Christ's example to serve

A dispute also arose among them as to which one of them was to be regarded as the greatest.…[Jesus] said to them … "The greatest among you must become like the youngest, and the leader like one who serves. For who is greater, the one who is at the table or the one who serves? Is it not the one at the table? But I am among you as one who serves" (Luke 22:24, 26, 27).

Even as we talk about loving and serving God through Jesus Christ, we often find ourselves vying with one another over who is the best. Perhaps we think that we love and serve God better than the person who was elected president of a charitable group of which we are a member. Or maybe we feel that we have more experience and expertise than someone who was assigned a new project or position.

We feel guilty about reacting this way, but we often can't help ourselves. So how are we going to handle it? We can use the situation to learn more about living and serving in the world. We can ask God to give us comfort and understanding. And, although it is very difficult, we can congratulate and support the person who has been chosen. We can ask God to give us the strength to be gracious and to serve.

After he had washed their feet, … [Jesus] said to them, "Do you know what I have done to you? You call me Teacher and Lord — and you are right, for that is what I am. So if I, your Lord and Teacher, have washed your feet, you also ought to wash one another's feet. For I have set you an example, that you also should do as I have done to you. Very truly, I tell you, servants are not greater than their master, nor are messengers greater than the one who sent them. If you know these things, you are blessed if you do them" (John 13:12–17).

By following Jesus' example, we can practise becoming the servant of others and, in so doing, know that we are serving God. If we find this a somewhat disappointing solution, we have only to remember in whose footsteps we are attempting to walk.

Prayer suggestions

- ∾ "Sometimes, Lord, I feel jealous that another person has been chosen to do a job that I think I could do better. Forgive me, Lord, for wanting to be seen as greater than others. Help me, Lord, to be willing to be a servant of others."
- ∾ "I am willing, Lord, to use the gift you have given me, in service to the group. Help me, Lord, not to impose my will on others but to guide the group to work together, in service one to another and to your glory."

Harvest of the Spirit
Preparing for a spiritual harvest

The fruit of the Spirit is love, joy, peace, patience, kindness, generosity, faithfulness, gentleness, and self-control. ... If we live by the Spirit, let us also be guided by the Spirit ... if you sow to the Spirit, you will reap eternal life from the Spirit (Galatians 5:22, 23, 25; 6:8).

If the Spirit is the source of our life, let the Spirit also direct our course.... If he sows in the field of the Spirit, the Spirit will bring him a harvest of eternal life (Galatians 5:25; 6:8, New English Bible translation).

The N.E.B. translation of sowing in the field of the spirit suggests a farming metaphor. The Holy Spirit is both the field and the harvest. Before the Spirit can give the harvest, there has to be preparation of the earth — clearing stones, pulling weeds, turning soil, watering ground. Nurturing the growth of the Spirit requires continual effort on our part — prayer and worship, self-study and meditation, good works and holy living. There may even be trials and tribulations, but

> ...Those who sow in tears reap with shouts of joy.
> Those who go out weeping, bearing the seed for sowing,
> shall come home with shouts of joy, carrying their sheaves
> (Psalm 126:6, 7).

How do we ensure a good harvest? First, we turn to the source of life, the Spirit, and ask daily for the good seed of the Holy Spirit to be planted in us; then we wait on the Spirit in prayer and meditation. We work in the field of the Spirit and prepare it to receive the seed.

Removing the stones and pulling out the weeds is like self-examination. We look into ourselves and attempt to see the things that hinder us from sowing the seed of the Spirit. Sometimes we find desires or thoughts that disturb us. When we discover these hindrances, we need to recognize them and accept them. They are real and, for the moment, they are part of us. When we acknowledge them, their power over us begins to dissolve, leaving us more able to deal with them and to follow the Spirit.

Turning the soil and watering the ground is like personal growth. We allow ourselves to take up healthy and fulfilling pursuits. We may spend time with God in reading or prayer; we may walk with God in a park or the country, by helping a friend in need, by making a special effort at work, or by providing help to a service organization. Anything that makes us feel wholesome and worthwhile is good nourishhment for the seed of the Spirit.

We cannot expect instant change, instant good harvest — old habits die hard. It is easy to get discouraged. We need to be gentle with ourselves and work the field one section at a time. We need to decide, with the guidance of the Spirit, which area to work first. Then we can put a small plan into action — name one thing to do this day, one thing to help us be happier, gentler, more loving.

Suggestions for preparation for the harvest

∾ If you want to be more loving, do one loving act each day for a week.

Give your child a hug and a smile
   for no reason.
Give a gift or a compliment
   to a co-worker.
Offer to babysit for your friend, so that she can
   get a break for a couple of hours.
Phone or visit a shut-in.

∾ After each loving action, thank the Spirit for helping you to prepare the field to receive the seed of love. Don't be disheartened if sometimes you seem to have let yourself down.

- Remember that you were successful in performing one loving action, and you can plan to do another loving action. It requires continual effort. You have to keep turning the soil, replacing old habits with new ones, pulling up weeds, throwing out stones.

Keep your mind on the positive thing you did and the
  progress you made today.
Keep yourself in step with the Spirit. One step at a time.
Remember to be gentle and loving with yourself.
Remember that you are not alone, that the Spirit is
  within you to guide you and help you.

Hands of Christ
Holding life in a sacred manner

Meditation

- "I come today to put myself in your hands, O Lord. I come to walk in your footsteps, see with your eyes, hear with your ears, and hold with your hands. When I hold life with your hands, I hold it in a sacred manner. I take hold of whatever is given me and grasp it as if it is holy."
  "I take this cup of water, as if from you. I hold this cup of water to give to someone, as if I were giving it to Jesus."

"I hold this child's hand, as if I were holding the hand of the child Jesus."

"I receive this gift from a friend, as if from God."

"I shake this person's hand, as if I were being introduced to Jesus."

"I wash this patient in my care, as if it were Jesus who was sick."

"I receive this bread from my host, as if Jesus were giving me bread at the Last Supper."

∿ If I perceive the person who is ministering to me or the person to whom I am ministering as Christ, all of life will be sanctified.

See the hands of Christ healing the sick.
See the hands of Christ blessing the people.
See the hands of Christ feeding the people.
See the hands of Christ washing the disciples' feet.

"I see Christ in my hands as I wash my ailing mother."
"I see Christ in my hands as I feed my family."

"Lord, help me to receive from others, as if from
    your hands."
"Lord, help me to give to others, as if by your hands."

I Am the Bread of Life

Christ feeds you in your spiritual hunger

In the desert God gave the Israelites manna to satisfy their physical needs.

> There on the surface of the wilderness was a fine flaky
> substance, as fine as frost on the ground. When the
> Israelites saw it, they said to one another, "What is it?"
> For they did not know what it was. Moses said to them,
> "It is the bread that the Lord has given you to eat. This is
> what the Lord has commanded: "Gather as much of it as
> each of you needs" … those who gathered much had

nothing over, and those who gathered little had no short-age; they gathered as much as each of them needed (Exodus 16:14–16, 18).

Jesus gives us the bread of life to satisfy our spiritual needs.

I am the bread of life. Your ancestors ate the manna in the wilderness, and they died. This is the bread that comes down from heaven, so that one may eat of it and not die. I am the living bread that came down from heaven. Whoever eats of this bread will live forever (John 6:48–51).

Daily we come to Christ to receive the bread of life. Our spiritual hunger is satisfied through his word, through prayer, through fellowship with one another, through communion at the Eucharist. Like the people who gathered as much manna as they needed for the physical body, we gather what our spiritual needs require. Those who gather much will have nothing left over, and those who gather little will have no shortage. Christ fills us with as much as we need to sustain our spiritual life.

When we have an extraordinary need, we ask for an extraordinary spiritual supply. And we can ask without hesitation, for we know that God, through Jesus the Christ, will give us what we need: "Whoever comes to me will never be hungry" (John 6:35).

Prayer suggestions

- ∾ Tell God your spiritual needs. Say the Lord's Prayer: "Give us this day our daily bread."

    ~ Accept God's supply for your spiritual need. Thank God for filling your need. Feel the calm and the joy at being satisfied with the bread of life.

I Am the Good Shepherd
Christ protects his flock

I am the good shepherd. The good shepherd lays down his life for the sheep (John 10:11).

Jesus is the shepherd, and we are his flock of sheep. We belong to him, and he will protect us against all that would harm us, even at the cost of his own life. We know that we can believe this passage, because this is what Christ did. He died on the cross to give us life.

In one of his parables (see Luke 15:3–7) Jesus said that, if the shepherd has one hundred sheep and one should get lost, he will leave the whole flock and go in search of the one that has strayed. If we lose our way and stray from the path where Christ is, we may find it difficult to get back to him. We may feel frightened or unworthy, and fear that God will never have anything to do with us again. But as soon as we realize what has happened and call out for help, God will answer our cry of need and rescue us. We will not be rejected or abandoned.

God is more willing to forgive than we are to ask forgiveness. God made us, God loves us, and God doesn't want to lose us. Jesus assures us that he will search us out and bring us back into the fold.

> *He will feed his flock like a shepherd; he will gather the lambs in his arms, and carry them in his bosom, and gently lead the mother sheep* (Isaiah 40:11).

Prayer suggestions

- "Good Shepherd, I am a member of your flock. I want to be with you, but sometimes I am tempted by other pastures and wander away. Lord, I ask you to forgive me."
- "Good Shepherd, when I am lost and can't find my way back to you, do not abandon me."
- "Jesus, Shepherd of the flock, search for me and find me. Bring me back to your fold in safety."

I Am the Light of the World

Christ lights your spiritual path

Again Jesus spoke to them, saying, "I am the light of the world. Whoever follows me will never walk in darkness but will have the light of life" (John 8:12).

In the country at night the darkness seems complete. When first we go outside, we feel that we could stretch out our hand and touch the darkness, as if it were a physical object. But if we stand and wait patiently, our eyes become accustomed to the dark, and we begin to see ever so faintly. Perhaps the stars are twinkling overhead or, between the clouds, the moon is shining through. Gradually we begin to perceive outlines and then objects, and soon we are able, with care, to find our way.

Christ tells us that he is the light of the world, the light of life. He says that he will not leave his followers in darkness. Even though we may be at a place in our life that appears pitch black, if we ask and wait patiently, Christ will light up each step of the way, illuminating the obstructions and pitfalls. His light will transform every difficulty encountered — spiritual, emotional, physical. It will shine on illness, bereavement, poverty, loneliness, and busyness, and help us to find our way through.

ꙮ "Lord, light of the world, light my way, so that I can pass safely through the dangers and live in you, the light of life."

I Am the Vine

Christ is the Vine, we are the branches

I am the vine, you are the branches. Those who abide in me and I in them bear much fruit, because apart from me you can do nothing (John 15:5).

At the beginning of the passage in which this verse appears, Jesus says that he is the true vine and that the Father is the gardener. The gardener cuts off branches that don't bear fruit and prunes branches that give grapes, so that they will bear even more fruit. We are to be branches of the true vine and to bear fruit. In order to come to our full potential, to give more and better quality fruit, we need to undergo pruning.

Throughout our lives we often discover that the same difficulties or frustrations repeatedly confront us. Perhaps we find ourselves becoming angry in situations when we thought we had conquered our tendency toward anger. Perhaps we thought that we had given ourselves completely into God's hands but find that we lack faith in a time of trial. Perhaps we thought that we had made a breakthrough into generosity but find that we are not sharing what we have with others.

These discoveries are as painful and as necessary as pruning is to the vine's branches. Each time we realize that we still become angry, we still lack faith, or we still need to learn generosity, the realization comes from the Father's pruning; and this pruning will strengthen the spiritual fruit.

> *The fruit of the Spirit is love, joy, peace, patience, kindness, generosity, faithfulness, gentleness, and self-control* (Galatians 5:22, 23).

Prayer suggestions

- ∾ "Lord Jesus, you have told us that you are the vine and we are the branches that produce the fruit of the Spirit."
- ∾ "Lord Jesus, you have told us that the Father is the gardener who prunes the branches that are dead or whose spiritual fruit is weak."
- ∾ "Lord Jesus, the spiritual fruit in me is becoming stronger daily through the Father's pruning of my branch within the vine."
- ∾ "Lord Jesus, help me not to be discouraged at the continual need for pruning; assist me to see that the spiritual fruit becomes stronger and more mature in you, the vine, each time the branch is pruned."

Incense

Prayer rises to God with the incense

Sometimes, when we sit or kneel in meditation, smouldering incense can help to bring us into God's presence. The sight of the smoke rising up and the pleasing aroma can assist us to lift our thoughts and prayers to God.

The sense of smell has the power to transport us to another time and place, in this case to the spiritual house of God. If we have no incense, we can use this verse from the psalms as an opening to our prayers:

> Let my prayer be counted as incense before you,
> and the lifting up of my hands as an evening sacrifice
> (Psalm 141:2).

In his vision, St. John saw the prayers of the saints and angels in heaven rising to God in the smoke of the incense:

> Another angel with a golden censer came and stood at the
> altar; he was given a great quantity of incense to offer
> with the prayers of all the saints on the golden altar that
> is before the throne. And the smoke of the incense, with
> the prayers of the saints, rose before God from the hand of
> the angel (Revelation 8:3, 4).

- Set up a prayer table, a candle, and some incense to be lit at your prayer time.
- Print out one of the above verses and read it before your prayer time.
- Watch the smoke of the incense (actual or imagined) rise up to God and see your prayers rise up with the smoke to God's throne.

Itinerary Prayers
Prayers for a safe journey

We think little about getting into a car and rushing off to the shops or the movies, or getting on a plane and travelling for business or pleasure. Yet when we hear news of car accidents or plane crashes, we are shocked; many of us know someone who has been in an accident.

A century ago travel was harder, and undertaken only after much preparation and forethought. If a monk left the abbey for any purpose, prayers were said for his safe journey and return.

Today I always make the sign of the cross when I get into the driver's seat. I pray to God for help to drive with care, so that I cause harm to no one and am kept safe myself. The prayer reminds me that I am in God's keeping. A friend of mine calls down her guardian angels to protect her whenever she gets into a car. She asks them to surround her car with light and guide her on her way.

One of the itinerary prayers in the *Monastic Diurnal*, a book of services used in some monasteries, asks that the angel Raphael go with us in our travels. In the book of Tobit in the Apocrypha, the story is told of Raphael in human form, accompanying Tobias on his journey to his kinsfolk. Tobias has many adventures but is protected through them all, and brought home in safety by the guidance and help of the angel Raphael.

Prayer suggestions

∾ Make a prayer ritual for safekeeping when you travel, to bring into remembrance that you are in God's care.

Ask God to be with you and protect you and others as you drive the car.
Say the Lord's Prayer and Psalm 23.
Use a prayer from The Book of Alternative Services of the Anglican Church of Canada; perhaps "For Those Who Travel," page 682, or "For a Member Leaving Home," page 696.

Jesus
Praying the name of Jesus

There are many ways to include the name of Jesus in your prayers. One way is to quiet your breathing and repeat the name, Jesus, in your mind and heart. Whenever you find yourself distracted, bring yourself quietly back to the name of Jesus.

People in the Orthodox church are encouraged to pray the "Jesus Prayer" continually throughout the day and night, in conjunction with the heart beat or the breath. Any of three versions are commonly used, one longer and two shorter.

Lord Jesus Christ, Son of the living God, have mercy
    on me, a sinner.
Or: Lord, have mercy.
Or: Jesus, mercy.

Praying the name of Jesus with a reading of scripture

∽ The name of Jesus can also be used in prayer together with a passage of scripture. This prayer has three parts:

1. Jesus before the eyes
Before you begin to read the Bible passage pray, "Jesus, Lord, help me to see you before my eyes in this Bible reading." Read the portion of scripture; then with Jesus before the eyes, consider what it is he is showing you in the reading.

2. Jesus in the heart
Now pray, "Jesus, Lord, come into my heart and abide with me today, in the way you have revealed yourself to me in the Bible reading." Sit quietly, allowing Jesus to be in the centre of your being.

3. Jesus in the hands
Now pray, "Jesus, Lord, manifest yourself through me this day. Give yourself to others through my actions, in the way you reveal yourself to me, and become present in my being through my Bible reading and meditation. Jesus, use my hands and my actions to show yourself to those with whom I come in contact today."

∽ Here is a scripture passage that I like to use when praying the name of Jesus:

Jesus took with him Peter and James and his brother John and led them up a high mountain, by themselves. And he

*was transfigured before them, and his face shone like the
sun, and his clothes became dazzling white. Suddenly
there appeared to them Moses and Elijah, talking with
him. Then Peter said to Jesus, "Lord, it is good for us to be
here; if you wish, I will make three dwellings here, one for
you, one for Moses, and one for Elijah." While he was
still speaking, suddenly a bright cloud overshadowed
them, and from the cloud a voice said, "This is my Son,
the Beloved; with him I am well pleased; listen to him!"
When the disciples heard this, they fell to the ground and
were overcome by fear. But Jesus came and touched them,
saying, "Get up and do not be afraid." And when they
looked up, they saw no one except Jesus himself alone*
(Matthew 17:1–8).

Joy
Joy in the Lord is your strength

*Go your way, eat the fat and drink sweet wine and send
portions of them to those for whom nothing is prepared,
for this day is holy to our Lord; and do not be grieved, for
the joy of the Lord is your strength* (Nehemiah 8:10).

Sometimes, we think that a serious and suffering demeanour is a
prerequisite for being Christian. But God tells us to celebrate,

eat good things, drink sweet wine, and invite others to share our happiness. God has given us what we need, and it is ours to share. When we give a gift, we receive joy; when we accept a gift, we receive joy also.

True joy, free and unalloyed, is a great gift. Probably many of us feel that it comes our way all too infrequently. When it does come, we may hesitate to enjoy it fully. Perhaps we feel guilty about being happy; there are so many people in the world who are unhappy. Perhaps we feel afraid about being joyful; there may be a price to pay for our good fortune.

But to cheat ourselves of the full and honest experience of joy is to deny the goodness and abundance of God our creator and sustainer. If we allow ourselves to fully experience the joy that comes from the goodness of God, then we will be strengthened to live more fully and to give ourselves more generously. The deeper we experience God's joy, the greater will be our capacity to share God's joy with others, and to spread God's joy abroad in the world.

Meditation

- ∾ "Joy in the Lord is my strength. I am refreshed and share with others. I cannot remain sad because joy in the Lord is my strength."
- ∾ "Lord, you are not asking a price for your gift — it is given freely. I receive your gift of joy with grateful thanks. I will share it."

*O children of Zion, be glad and rejoice in the Lord your
God; for he has given the early rain for your vindication,
he has poured down for you abundant rain, the early and
the later rain, as before* (Joel 2:23).

*When the Lord restored the fortunes of Zion,
we were like those who dream.
Then our mouth was filled with laughter,
and our tongue with shouts of joy* (Psalm 126:1, 2).

Kingdom of Heaven
Possessing the kingdom
now and in the future

The kingdom of heaven is portrayed in the Bible as a state of being that we can possess now, as well as a life that will be given to us in the future.

> *Again, the kingdom of heaven is like a merchant in search of fine pearls; on finding one pearl of great value, he went and sold all that he had and bought it (Matthew 13:45–46).*

> *The kingdom of God is among you (Luke 17:21).*

The kingdom of heaven is a state of living with Jesus, a state of being in his presence at all times. God gives this kingdom with no strings attached, but we have to take hold of it ourselves. It is present among us, but we have to reach out and accept it.

We can find the kingdom, the pearl of great value, and ignore it. Or we can find the kingdom, realize that it is worth more than anything else in our possession, and accept it as our own, even if this means giving up everything else we have.

I imagine that the merchant in the parable had been buying pearls for a long time; so he knew how to calculate their value. When he saw this special pearl, he knew right away that it was worth more than anything else in his possession, and he sold all the others in order to buy this one. The merchant knew that he was getting the best of the bargain. The merchant could have said that he would rather have a large number of pearls even though their value could not match the one special pearl. They would look good in a display, and he would gain notice as a collector. He could have opted for quantity instead of quality. But he knew that, in this one pearl, he had more beauty and value than he had ever owned before.

There is no need for us to be afraid to give up our pearls of lesser value for one pearl of quality, because in this one special pearl we have the best, all that we will ever need. There are so many things in life that we think we could not do without. But are they really of the highest quality? Do they really help us to live in God's kingdom? Are they of genuine value in our quest to grow in spirit and serve in the world?

Holding on to an old way of life may prevent us from accepting the new treasure. We have to let go of the things that hold us back from God, so that our hands are free to accept the kingdom. Then, seeming to possess nothing, we have everything.

Strive for his kingdom, and these things will be given to you as well (Luke 12:31).

Prayer suggestions

∞ "Lord, you have told me that, if I first strive for the kingdom of heaven, the pearl of great value, I will live more abundantly."

∞ "Lord, I know that, to accept the gift of your kingdom, I must let go of unworthy distractions and be open to you."

∞ "Lord, through your grace I have found the kingdom of heaven — the pearl of great value. Thank you, Lord, for this gift."

Knock
Your act of knocking opens the spiritual door

Knock, and the door will be opened for you.... For everyone who knocks, the door will be opened (Luke 11:9, 10).

Lift up your heads, O gates!
and be lifted up, O ancient doors!
that the King of glory may come in (Psalm 24:7).

(Also helpful are Luke 11:5-10; Matthew 7, 8; John 10:1–10.)

There are doors in our lives that separate us from God. They are doors of our own making. This room is sacred, we say; this room is secular. In this room I talk to God; in this room I talk to my friends. In this space I do God's work; in this area I work for myself.

When we knock on these doors, it is as if we were knocking from the inside. The very act of knocking causes the doors to open, so that communication between God and us becomes easy and natural. The division between sacred and secular is removed. Christ waits for the knock that signifies our desire to include him in our lives.

All sorts of wonderful things happen when the doors open and life becomes one, lived in God. Sometimes these things are so amazing that we call them coincidences, luck, flukes. They are God's gifts, God's presence, God's joy, God's voice. But we need to recognize them as coming from God, or else we shut the door again.

God's gifts are freely given; they are not trade-offs — a good thing now for suffering later. Yet suffering inevitably comes, and sometimes we say that it is God's will. But God does not will suffering, nor does God impose suffering on us as punishment. Suffering is built into being human, being animal, being on earth. You catch a virus and get sick; you trip on the sidewalk, fall down, and break a bone; you eat too many green apples, and you get an upset stomach. These are natural causes and consequences.

But if we keep the door open, God leads us through times of difficulty and suffering. In fact, Jesus said of himself that he is the door, the gate, the way through:

I am the gate for the sheep.... Whoever enters by me will be saved, and will come in and go out and find pasture (John 10:7, 9).

Prayer suggestions

- ∾ "Lord, there are doors that separate my life into sacred and secular. I want to live my life with you, with no barrier between us. Lord, I knock on a door of separation. Let the door open."

- ∾ Choose an area of your life that doesn't seem to involve God, like doing the laundry. Say something like: "Lord, here I am doing the laundry. We can talk."

- ∾ You would be thinking of things while you were doing the laundry, so just share them with God. "I'm worried about Jimmy. I haven't had a letter from him for a while. I hope he's all right. God, please take care of him."

- ∾ Next time something good happens to you, say, "Thank you, God."

- ∾ Next time something bad happens to you, you could say, "God, walk with me, carry me, hold my hand — whatever it takes to get me through this. I believe you have only my good in mind. Thank you, God."

Life
Choose life, love God

I have set before you life and death.... Choose life
(Deuteronomy 30:19).

I came that they may have life, and have it abundantly
(John 10:10).

In the book of Deuteronomy we read that God gave the Israelites
a choice. He set before them life and death and curses, and told
them to choose life. God told them that, by choosing to love and
obey him, they would live long in the promised land. God gave
them a land full of good things, a land flowing with milk and
honey. With all this before them, how could they refuse to love

and obey him? He promised them that, if they held him close, if they chose to love him, they would continue to live life to its fullest.

As God gave the land and promise of abundant life to the Israelites, God has also given the promise of life to us in his son Jesus, the Christ.

We wonder at the stories of the Israelites falling away from loving and serving God, when they knew that their reward for keeping faith with him would be fullness of life. And yet we find ourselves in the same position. We know that, when we love God and live in Christ, our lives will be abundant and full. But we chase after other pleasures and accomplishments and are surprised when, in the end, they don't satisfy us.

We needn't be afraid that, if we love God in Jesus, God will take away everything else from us, will deny us everything else. No. When we put the love of God first, we will enjoy fullness of life in all things.

Prayer suggestions

- ∞ "Jesus, Lord, you came to earth and showed me how to live life to its fullest. I thank you, Lord, for this full life you offer me."
- ∞ "Lord, I accept this life you give to me. I know that you do not deny me other good things in life. Lord, I accept all these other gifts from you and enjoy them in your name."

Every perfect gift is from above, coming down from the Father of lights (James 1:17).

Listen

Speak, Lord, your servant is listening

The boy Samuel was ministering to the Lord under Eli.... The lamp of God had not yet gone out, and Samuel was lying down in the temple of the Lord, where the ark of God was. Then the Lord called, "Samuel! Samuel!" and he said, "Here I am!" and ran to Eli, and said, "Here I am, for you called me." But he said, "I did not call; lie down again." So he went and lay down. The Lord called again, "Samuel!" Samuel got up and went to Eli and said, "Here I am, for you called me." But he said, "I did not call, my son; lie down again." Now Samuel did not yet know the Lord, and the word of the Lord had not yet been revealed to him. The Lord called Samuel again, a third time. And he got up and went to Eli, and said, "Here I am, for you called me." Then Eli perceived that the Lord was calling the boy. Therefore Eli said to Samuel, "Go, lie down; and if he calls you, you shall say, 'Speak, Lord, for your servant is listening.'" So Samuel went and lay down in his place. Now the Lord came and stood there, calling as before, "Samuel! Samuel!" And Samuel said, "Speak, for your servant is listening" (1 Samuel 3:1, 3–10).

There are so many voices in the world and so many needs. They call us this way and that until we become confused and exhausted. We may respond to such a lot of needs that we can't hear the

Lord's voice anymore, or we hear the voice but don't recognize it. The voice seems to be just another one of our "Elis" — one of our many deserving people or organizations. We need time and space to listen for a while until we can say, "Speak, Lord, for your servant is listening."

"Now Samuel did not yet know the Lord." Like Samuel, when we listen, we may hear a deeper message. Good works are fine — the world would be lost without them. Many people do good works, but they don't all know the Lord. Yet God is the source of all good works, and God calls us to be partners in the work. God is also the source of the strength to do the work. If we are replenished by the grace of God, our good works will further the kingdom of God.

We need to take time to listen. We can spend a few minutes each day, a morning or afternoon, or a weekend's retreat. We need a quiet place — a room in our home, a pew in a church. The silence may seem scary at first. Or it may seem as if we're being lazy and irresponsible. If we're used to filling our days with busyness — phone calls, shopping, reading a magazine, feeding the family, walking the dog, seeing a friend — time with nothing to do can cause all kinds of guilt. But if we continue to sit and listen, the silence grows into a healing presence that gives us the strength to do what we have to do. When various concerns intrude and we think of things we should do, we can write them down, so that we won't forget them, and then we can continue in silence.

We may get to the point where we feel that we can't be quiet any longer, or that it's just not working, or that nothing's happening. When this time comes, it's worth trying five more minutes. This is often the critical moment when the Lord breaks through our barriers. When this happens, there is new energy, a sense of calm, and a renewed ability to get on with the things that need to be done.

Prayer suggestions

- ✺ Put aside half an hour to stop and listen to God. Unplug the phone, so that its ringing doesn't distract you. Take your half-hour while there's no one around to interrupt you. If that's not possible, tell people in your home that you will not be available for half an hour. If necessary, hang a "not to be disturbed" sign on your door.
- ✺ Hear God's voice saying, "Be still and know that I am God." Respond to God by saying, "Speak Lord, your servant is listening."
- ✺ In a journal, write down what you felt or heard God saying to you. Write down your response to God's voice.

Love in Action
Love your neighbour as yourself

How does God's love abide in anyone who has the world's goods and sees a brother or sister in need and yet refuses help? Little children, let us love, not in word or speech, but in truth and action (1 John 3:17, 18).

When you reap the harvest of your land, you shall not reap to the very edges of your field, or gather the gleanings of your harvest; you shall leave them for the poor and for the alien (Leviticus 23:22).

The first commandment is to love God with all your heart, all your mind, and all your strength. Jesus says that the second commandment is like it: love your neighbour as yourself. (See Matthew 22:38 and Mark 12:28.)

It is easy to say that we love God. Who can question it? We go to church, say our prayers, know our Bible, maybe sing in the church choir. But prayers and church attendance are only one side of the coin. The other side is love in action. If the love of God abides in us, thoughts and acts of kindness become second nature — God's nature working in us. We share our bounty with others, we leave the gleanings of our field for those who are poor. We offer supporting words to a family member, we are considerate toward a store clerk, we phone or visit a lonely person, we buy an extra tin of vegetables for the food bank, or we give an hour of our time to volunteer in some capacity.

Prayer suggestions

∿ "Lord, help me to love you in word.
   Lord, help me to love you in deed."
∿ "Thank you for your love that lives in me.
   Help me to share your love with others."
∿ "I believe your gifts to me include (list some of your gifts; for example, literacy, time, a vegetable garden). I promise to share one of your gifts to me with someone who needs it.

"I will help someone to read."

"I will give an hour of my time to help someone."

"I will share my vegetables with someone who doesn't have much to eat."

∞ "Thank you for showing me how to put your love in action. Help me to carry it through."

Love of God Seeks Us

God's love wants only your good

The love of God seeks us in every situation, and seeks our good. His inscrutable love seeks our awakening (Thomas Merton, New Seeds of Contemplation).

To know that the love of God seeks our good in every situation is a wonderful support. Just think about it — no matter what happens to us, God wants only to give us what is best in that situation. So God and we are in accord. God wants what is best for us, and we want what is best for us.

Sometimes, like Adam and Eve (see Genesis 3:8–10), we try to hide from God. God says, "Where are you?" and we respond, "I heard you coming and I hid from you." When we wander away from God, God seeks us to draw us back. Occasionally God has to resort to dramatic means to get our attention. Moses saw a bush that was on fire but not consumed by the flames; Paul was blinded by a bright light from heaven and heard God's voice; St. Francis of Assisi, a rich man, sat alone in an empty church and was shown that he must become poor for Christ's sake; John Wesley entered a religious meeting house to get out of the cold and heard God speaking to him.

Prayer suggestions

- When you are calm and collected, read Exodus 3:2–4 or Acts 9:1–9.
- Think of your own life. Is God seeking you through some means, as he sought Moses and Paul? Ask God to open your eyes to see his leading. Thank God for seeking after you and finding you.

Meditation and Contemplation

*Thinking about God and gazing upon him
in spiritual wonder*

*Seek the Lord and his strength;
seek his presence continually* (Psalm 105:4).

Look to him, and be radiant (Psalm 34:5).

*I will call to mind the deeds of the Lord;
I will remember your wonders of old.
I will meditate on all your work,
and muse on your mighty deeds* (Psalm 77:11, 12).

Meditation and contemplation are two words that describe similar types of prayer and are often used interchangeably. But there is a distinction. When meditating, we turn an idea or an episode over in our mind, looking for insights or connections within the subject of meditation itself, or between the subject and our experience. When contemplating, we hold a single idea or word or image in our mind without actively thinking about it, simply letting it be and waiting for a gift of comprehension or understanding to come to us. Both types of prayer help us to draw closer to God. Through them we discover more about God's attributes and God's purpose for our lives. We also learn more about ourselves and our world.

Aids to meditation and contemplation

Reading a passage from the Bible or other spiritual book is a good way to prepare for meditation or contemplation. If you read it before bed, your mind and heart can work with it while you sleep. In the morning, just recall the reading, and then ask God to reveal himself to you.

If you are meditating, you can think about the meaning of the passage — how it reveals God to you, how it connects with you, what it asks of you. You gently examine it from different angles. You may find that your mind continues to work on the passage while you are engaged in other completely different activities, and that a new realization about the passage may suddenly surface later on.

If you are contemplating, you can select a single element from the passage, gazing on this particular picture of God as an infant looks up at the face of the one who is holding him. There is complete trust as you rest in God's arms. You see only God, nothing else matters, everything fades into the background. You need no explanation of God's love; you just accept it.

An important part of both meditation and contemplation is making a record of your discoveries in a diary or journal. The session is not really complete until you have objectified the results in this way. Recording your discoveries in writing or drawing (or in a computer file) has the effect of anchoring them in your experience, so that they are not lost but endure and enrich your future thought, feeling, and action.

Miracles
Everyday occurrences are miracles

Is the rising of the sun each morning an ordinary event? Is it ordinary that an animal produces milk for her young? These are everyday miracles. We are so used to them that they may seem ordinary, but are they anything short of amazing?

And what of the involuntary act of breathing? Our lungs extract oxygen from the air, the blood carries the oxygen around the body, giving life to the cells, then returns to the lungs, which exhale the carbon dioxide. This is surely miraculous.

We tend to be unaware of the miracles around us and inside us until an interruption intervenes, such as a bodily illness or a natural disaster. Then we say, "How could this have happened?" It is only when a miracle is impaired that we are mindful of the miracle at all. Of course, God doesn't send us difficulties or deprivations in order to make us aware of the miraculous in the ordinary, but we can use difficulties and deprivations to recall the amazing events that go on all the time.

Prayer suggestions

∽ Look for miracles in your day-to-day life. Write down five things that you count as miracles; for example, fresh water, sight, literacy, hearing, health. Thank God for these miracles.

∽ Write down five things that you count as deprivations; for example, illness, power outage, eye problems, heat, cold, rain. Do they make you aware of miracles that you have taken for granted; for example, good health, electricity, sight, good weather?

∽ Thank God for the everyday miracles in your life.

Music
Finding God through music

Whenever the evil spirit from God came upon Saul, David took the lyre and played it with his hand, and Saul would be relieved and feel better, and the evil spirit would depart from him (1 Samuel 16:23).

I have had great refreshment of body, mind and spirit from the playing of this delightful complete instrument [guitar]. ... I write with experience of the benefits derived from such a hobby. One of my pupils had that distressing malady, St. Vitus' Dance, but after three years of learning to control her movements by playing a musical instrument, and helped by the soothing tones of the music itself, all trace of this complaint vanished (article in Guitar News *by O.M. Lawrence*).

My father wrote this article in *Guitar News*. I have fond memories of falling asleep to the sound of his music.

Music can sooth the mind and the spirit and enable healing. In Type 2 Diabetes, the glucose in the blood can't get into the cells to produce energy because there is insufficient insulin to unlock the cells' receptors. Exercise helps to activate the receptors of insulin to open the cells' locks, and a good way to exercise is to walk to music. Music provides rhythm for the feet. Our feet hear the music through the beat, and our body and spirit respond.

Music can also help us in prayer. It helps the spirit and mind to soar. Plainsong or Gregorian chant sung by a church choir lifts us out of ordinary life and into the extraordinary world of the spirit. It puts us in touch with God.

Music doesn't have to be religious in order to lift the spirit up to heaven. We can use sound tracks from movies, instrumental music, choral music, and simple love songs.

Prayer suggestion

∾ Choose some music that you like. Let your spirit soar in prayer to God.

New

Renewal of the spirit through the winter of the soul

The Protestant work ethic insists that idle hands find evil work. Consequently, we find it difficult to take time out and rest. But we need to remember that we lose a lot in life by not taking the time to stop and ponder God's glory.

Winter is a time of rest for lands and forests before they wake up with new life in spring. Our bodies need the rest provided by sleep during the night. Our inner life — the life of the soul — needs rest periods too, its "winter" or "night," when it regains energy and is renewed. These are the times when we may feel sluggish about prayer, when our meditation seems to be getting nowhere. Attempting to force prayer and meditation are of little use. The inner life needs time to rest. We must have our blue days, down days, grey days — whatever we call them — as days given for the soul's rest.

Maybe we need a holiday away or a quiet time at home. Unfortunately, in the modern world we tend to make even our holidays into busy times. We may rush away somewhere and, when we get there, fill our moments with working at play. We shop and sightsee, play tennis or golf, go to a concert or movie, overeat, and when our holiday is over, we rush back home to continue our regular life and work. And nothing has changed. We have not allowed the soul to have the winter it needs to renew itself.

Perhaps we have been afraid to let our souls have their winter, afraid that spring will never come. But our souls, as well as our bodies, are part of the order of nature created by God. It is just as natural for our souls to have their winter of rest, as it is natural for them to enjoy again their spring of renewal.

Spring is a time of new beginnings, the greening time of earth, the time of growth. The trees show their aura — silver-white, soft green, subdued magenta. There are sudden bursts of glory, of thunder and lightning, as warm air meets cold. The plants of the forest's understorey take full advantage of the sun's light and the spring rains. The trout lilies, the spring beauties, the trillium, all spear through last year's fallen leaves and reach toward the sun, their source of energy. In a few days yellow, pink, white, and red punctuate the forest floor, and each flower sings a song of praise to God. So it is with our inner life — after the winter, a glorious spring will emerge.

Prayer suggestions

∽ On a winter of the soul day, recognize your soul's need to rest. Read a book, sit and stare, lie down and sleep. Ask God to prepare you for the new life he gives you.

∽ Thank God for the seasons of the soul.

The steadfast love of the Lord never ceases, his mercies never come to an end; they are new every morning (Lamentations 3:22, 23).

Offering
Giving the gift of yourself to Christ

When you are offering your gift at the altar, if you remem-
ber that your brother or sister has something against you,
leave your gift there before the altar and go; first be
reconciled to your brother or sister, and then come and
offer your gift (Matthew 5:23, 24).

When we offer God the gift of ourselves, we first look into our
heart to make sure our gift is pure. Perhaps we find that we have
wronged someone or hurt someone. We know that before we can
give ourselves completely to God, we must ask the person's forgiveness and be reconciled. Perhaps we can't meet with the wronged
person immediately, but we can promise God that, through God's
grace, we will work toward reconciliation with the person.

The same is true when we have wronged or hurt ourselves. The sorrow and anger, the frustration and guilt, will come between us and our good intentions toward ourselves and others if we cannot first forgive ourselves. Perhaps we can't completely eradicate the feelings of self-blame, but we can promise God that, through God's grace, we will work toward reconciliation with ourselves.

Then we can leave the gift of ourselves before God, knowing that it will be accepted as a pure gift. Of course, we will follow through on our promise of reconciliation. There can be no pretence.

Laid on the altar, O my Lord divine,
Accept this gift today for Jesus' sake;
I have no jewels to adorn thy shrine,
Nor any world-famed sacrifice to make.
But here I bring within my trembling hands
This will of mine — a thing that seemeth small —
And thou alone, O Lord, canst understand
How when I yield thee this, I yield thee all
(Source unknown).

When we give of ourselves or our substance, we are expressing the image of God within us. Giving is a primary characteristic of the divine nature. God gave the creation, and God gave the Son. Jesus gave healing, and Jesus gave himself. When we forgive others and ourselves, or give to those less fortunate than ourselves, we are following in the footsteps of Jesus.

The Bible tells us that all people are made in the image of God. By giving to others, therefore, we are returning what we have received through the bounty of God back to God. We are participating in the rich exchange of gifts that characterizes the God who gave in the creation, and the Son who gave for our redemption. Jesus tells us that this is especially true when we give to those in need.

> *"Lord, when was it that we saw you hungry and gave you food, or thirsty and gave you something to drink? And when was it that we saw you a stranger and welcomed you, or naked and gave you clothing? And when was it that we saw you sick or in prison and visited you?" And the king will answer them, "Truly I tell you, just as you did it to one of the least of these who are members of my family, you did it to me"* (Matthew 25:37–40).

The people in this story told by Jesus did not make a big show of what they were doing. Often people who do good things are not aware that they are doing anything out of the ordinary. What they do for others, they do for God. What they do for God, they do for others. There is no separation in their lives. Their offering to God and the creation is all one.

Prayer suggestions

- ∾ "Lord, I offer the gift of myself to you."
- ∾ "Lord, I have been reconciled with all those I know I have wronged."
- ∾ "Lord, I ask you to forgive me for these wrongs."
- ∾ "Lord, I offer the gift of myself to others."

Practice of the Presence of God

Being aware of God's presence with you at all times

Seek his presence continually (Psalm 105:4).

All the time, in work and prayer, in good times and bad, in everything, God is with us. We can practise being aware of God's presence. I say "practise" because we must use conscious effort to increase our awareness of God's presence. As we would practise playing the piano to improve our skill, so we need to practise being aware of God's presence until the activity becomes habitual for us.

In order to form a habit of conversing with God continu-
ally, and referring all we do to him, we must at first apply
to him with some diligence: but ... after a little care we
should find his love inwardly excite us to it without any
difficulty (Brother Lawrence, Practice of the Presence of
God*).*

In the seventeenth century a French monk named Brother Lawrence made this practice his life's goal. Although he did not wish
even to talk about his way of life, one person prevailed upon
him to reveal it. Lawrence agreed on condition that what he said
would not be repeated to anyone else. The promise was kept
until Lawrence's death, when the conversations and letters were
compiled. We have them today under the title, *The Practice of*
the Presence of God: The Best Rule of a Holy Life.

God is with us always, in good times and in bad. We can talk
to God as a constant companion who loves and understands us.
When we put matters into God's hands, God shares our respon-
sibility for them and we can let go of worry. Instead of fretting,
we can do what we have to do to the best of our ability, understanding that God will take care of the outcome.

As he proceeded in his work, he continued his familiar
conversation with his Maker, imploring his grace, and
offering to him all his actions. When he had finished, he
examined himself how he had discharged his duty; if he
found well, he returned thanks to God; if otherwise, he
asked pardon; and without being discouraged, he set his
mind right again and continued his exercise of the pres-
ence of God, as if he had never deviated from it (Brother
Lawrence, Practice of the Presence of God*).*

We often feel guilty when doing something we like. But we can tell God that we enjoy it, and receive what we're doing as a gift from God. When we were children and our mother gave us something to do that we liked, we did it with a glad heart and said, "Thanks, Mum. I really enjoyed that." If she gave us something we didn't like doing, we may have avoided it or done it quickly to get it over with. We might have said, "I don't think I'm ready for this," and she might have replied, "Try it and see how you get on. I'll help you if you need help" or "I'll ask your brother to help you."

We can speak with God as simply and easily as we would speak with a beloved parent, sharing our concerns and pleasures and knowing that God will do what is best for us. This may seem odd to us at first, especially if we think of God as immeasurably above and beyond us. But Jesus called God Abba, Father, demonstrating the intimate relationship between God and us, the children of God.

> *Rejoice always, pray without ceasing, give thanks in all circumstances; for this is the will of God in Christ Jesus for you* (1 Thessalonians 5:16–18).

Prayer suggestions

- ∾ "Lord, I want to learn to converse with you at all times. I want to share my whole life with you — my times of work and play as well as my times of prayer."
- ∾ "I know that when I do all you ask with you beside me and within me, I will not have to worry about the outcome. If I fail in some matter, I have only to ask forgiveness, and I can proceed in your presence with no more worry."

∾ "Lord, help me remember that you are always with me, my constant companion and friend."

Praying in Secret
Being alone with God

Our Lord was well versed in the scriptures and adhered to the rites of the Hebrew religion, but he did not like to make a public spectacle of his faith. He told his disciples that, when they prayed, they should not imitate the hypocrites.

> They love to stand and pray in the synagogues and at the street corners, so that they may be seen by others. Truly I tell you, they have received their reward. But whenever you pray, go into your room and shut the door and pray to your Father who is in secret; and your Father who sees in secret will reward you (Matthew 6:5, 6).

It is a human failing to want to be seen doing the right thing. What the "hypocrites" did when no one was watching, we don't know. But Christ tells us that no one except God needs to see our spiritual practice.

Jesus prayed in secret. He was an itinerant teacher who wandered around the countryside with his disciples delivering his message. But it is recorded in the gospels that he went apart from the crowd, and even from his disciples, to pray.

At the beginning of his ministry, immediately after he was baptized by John in the desert, "the heavens were opened to him and he saw the Spirit of God descending like a dove and alighting on him. And a voice from heaven said, 'This is my Son, the Beloved, with whom I am well pleased'" (Matthew 3:16, 17).

Then we read that the Spirit led him out into the wilderness where he fasted forty days and forty nights. Jesus had received the call and an outward sign of his vocation, and he could have gone at once into his ministry. But he chose instead to take a kind of retreat in the wilderness. The gospels tell us that during this retreat, as he considered his options, he was tempted by the devil.

Then after three years of ministry, on the night of his betrayal, he took his disciples to the Garden of Gethsemane. He asked them to wait and stay awake while he prayed. "Going a little farther, he threw himself on the ground and prayed" (Matthew 26:39).

By Christ's instruction and example we are, from time to time, to pray alone. We go apart from the crowd to hear God's voice. We go to church to worship God with others, to receive the sacraments, to listen to the scriptures and others' interpretation of the scriptures. But we need time apart from even religious things. We need to enter into our private room, shut the door, and pray to the God who is in that secret place. Then we can really hear "the still small voice," "the gentle whisper," or the "sound of sheer silence" in which Elijah heard what God wanted of him.

> *There was a great wind, so strong that it was splitting mountains and breaking rocks in pieces before the Lord, but the Lord was not in the wind; and after the wind an earthquake, but the Lord was not in the earthquake; and after the earthquake a fire, but the Lord was not in the fire; and after the fire a sound of sheer silence. When Elijah heard it, he wrapped his face in his mantle and went out and stood at the entrance of the cave. Then there came a voice to him ...* (1 Kings 19:11–13).

Prayer suggestions

- "Lord, I come to this quiet place where you alone can see me. In this place I am alone with you."
- "In this place of sheer silence I listen for your voice. I hear your voice in the silence saying, 'Who will go for me?' Lord, here am I, send me."

Quietness

In order to hear God's voice you need to be quiet

There is so much noise in our lives today. We are so busy doing that it's often hard just *to be* — to be quiet by ourselves, to be quiet with God, to sit and do nothing. God's voice is heard in silence.

Suggested actions

- Sit comfortably and close your eyes. Hold your hands in your lap. Breathe quietly and steadily. Repeat one of these phrases:

  "Be still and know that I am God."
  "In quietness and confidence shall be your strength."
  "Breathe on me, breath of God."

  or pray a familiar prayer or psalm.

∾ After a few repetitions, you will find that the phrases seem to repeat themselves in the background of your mind. It is like being by a lake and sitting with your eyes closed. You can hear the water lapping on the shore, but it is a background sound, and the front part of your mind can think of other things. Repeating a phrase or a prayer over and over helps, like the sound of the water lapping, to still the front part of your mind and open you to God's presence.

∾ There may be times in the stillness and quietness when you feel that you are holding all the cares of the world in your arms without any feeling of burden. This is a special form of supplication. You do not ask in words; you just bring people with you into God's presence, so that they receive the same blessings of peace that you receive yourself.

∾ At times, you may have a sense of knowing what God wants of you, though you have heard no words. You will always come away from this prayer feeling strengthened in his love and peace.

∾ You don't need to bring any agenda to this prayer. Just come. The rhythm of the phrase continues in the back of your mind while the front part of your mind is still, expectant, quiet. Even five or ten minutes spent with God in this manner gives strength and peace.

Ready
Being ready for Christ's return

Be dressed for action and have your lamps lit; be like those who are waiting for their master to return from the wedding banquet, so that they may open the door for him as soon as he comes and knocks ... be ready, for the Son of Man is coming at an unexpected hour (Luke 12:35, 36, 40).

Am I ready, Lord, if you should come? Am I ready to receive you in my heart? Am I dressed and ready for action with my lamp lit? What does it mean to be ready for your return? You are always with me.

The literal translation for the word *return* is "turn again." To be ready for the Lord's return is to be in a state of readiness to follow a new path.

We may have followed a certain path for a long time, but if Christ indicates a new road, we need to be ready to take it. When he knocks at the door, we need to be ready to open it. When a new way opens up, we may be taken by surprise. If we're not ready for the journey with our lamps lit, we might stumble and fall on the path. If we're prepared, we won't be hesitant to follow him, even when he asks us to do something that we've never done before. If our lamps are lit by regular prayer, we'll be ready to check out a new path and know whether it is his way for us or not.

In Jesus' parable, the ten bridesmaids went out to meet the bridegroom who was expected soon. They waited a long time and got drowsy and fell asleep. When the shout went up at midnight that the bridegroom was approaching, the bridesmaids got up and trimmed their lamps. Five of them had not brought any oil, and their lamps were going out. They asked the other five to give them some of their oil to replenish their lamps. You might expect the parable to be about generosity — the five wise bridesmaids would share what they had with the five foolish ones.

But there is a twist to the story. The wise bridesmaids refused the request and advised the others to go and buy oil from a merchant for, if they shared what they had, none of them would have enough. Generosity, in this case, would not have been wise. So the wise bridesmaids followed the bridegroom into the wedding banquet while the others went to get more oil. When they returned, they found the door to the feast shut, and the bridegroom refused to open it for them. They had missed their chance.

We must be ready for Christ's call to us by listening and praying to him. This is the oil that keeps the flame burning.

∾ "I am ready, Lord, for your return. By reading your word, I am dressed and ready to follow your lead. By prayer, my lamp is kept lit, and the jar of oil is kept full."

∾ "If I fall asleep while I wait for your new calling, I am ready to jump up and open the door at your knock."

∾ "Keep me ever alert to your return. Let me always be ready for your leading in new paths."

Retreats

How to benefit from a retreat when you return to your regular life

Sometimes we just want to get away from it all. It may be the winter with its cold, snow, and ice; the job with its overwhelming weight of work or boredom; the church, family, friends, or volunteer organizations.

> *O that I had wings like a dove!*
> *I would fly away and be at rest;*
> *truly, I would flee far away;*
> *I would lodge in the wilderness.*
> *I would hurry to find a shelter*
> *for myself from the raging wind and tempest*
> (Psalm 55:7–9).

So we make the break, take a holiday, make an old-fashioned retreat or quiet day, and it feels very good. But when it's all over, what then? When we get back from our vacation or retreat, the "same old same old" is still there.

In fact, it may feel worse than before because now we're more aware of how good life can be without the daily tensions and struggles. It is like a March storm that hits just as the snow has almost gone. We had thought that spring was nearly here. We had seen signs of spring in the greening grass, so instead of being glad of the short respite from winter, we are angry or dispirited when winter weather returns.

Are we better or worse off for having a vacation in a warm spot? Are we better or worse off for having a taste of spring? Are we better or worse off for having a retreat? It depends on whether we allow the taste of joy to carry over into our lives, or whether we become resentful after the respite.

After a time of quiet or listening, a retreat or a vacation, we need to prepare for our return to ordinary life. There are things we can do to help us keep the new spirit of peace in the old situations to which we return.

Suggestions

- At the end of your retreat or vacation, make notes of what you liked the most; for example, time alone, a chance to read, no phone calls.
- Make notes of any insights you had about your life, any messages from God.

∾ Perhaps you might like to keep a regular journal that includes helpful thoughts. You may want to record your dreams in it — daydreams and night dreams.

∾ Make notes of one or two things you would like to do daily when you return to your regular life. For exmple:

take five or ten minutes each day to be quiet;
unplug the phone for half an hour;
light a candle, perhaps some incense;
listen to music that lifts your spirit;
read the psalms, the Bible, a spiritually renewing book;
start a journal.

∾ If you feel down, look back at the notes you made when you were on retreat, remind yourself of your decisions, and recommit to them.

Creativity is God's energy flowing through us, shaped by us, like light flowing through a crystal prism. When we are clear about who we are and what we are doing, the energy flows freely and we experience no strain (Julia Cameron, The Artist's Way).

River of Water
The river of life
flows through the city street

Then the angel showed me the river of the water of life,
bright as crystal, flowing from the throne of God and of
the Lamb through the middle of the street of the city
(Revelation 22:1).

This description of the river "bright as crystal" conjures up an image of a pure life-giving stream that issues from God, the source of all life, and flows through the middle of the city's street.

St. John tells us that we can find God's creative flow not just in the pastoral scene where the Lord promised to lead his sheep beside still waters, but even in the busiest thoroughfare of the largest metropolis. Julia Cameron calls it "the flow of grace." It is the current that moves us to our rightful place in life.

This current, or river, is a flow of grace moving us to our
right livelihood, companions, destiny. Recovering is the
process of finding the river and saying yes to its flow,
rapids and all (Julia Cameron, The Artist's Way).

The passage in the Book of Revelation goes on to say,

On either side of the river is the tree of life with its twelve
kinds of fruit, producing its fruit each month; and the
leaves of the tree are for the healing of the nations
(Revelation 22:2).

No matter on which side of the river we are, we will find God's tree of life. No matter at what time of the year we come to this tree of life, we will find it in leaf and with fruit. Whenever we come to the tree of life we will be nourished and healed.

If we find ourselves by some other river, one that is polluted or full of debris, we will want to search for the river of life again. This is what Julia Cameron calls the recovering process.

Suggestions

∽ You will know that you are not by the river of the water of life when you feel bogged down, lacking in spirit, empty, troubled. To find the river of life again, you need

quiet time,
prayer time,
retreat time,
time for spiritual reading.

∽ When you have found your way back to the river of life,

sit on the bank of the river, in the shade of the tree of life,
eat of its fruit and be nourished,
take the leaves and be healed.

Then say, "Yes, Lord, I am ready to be in the flow of the river that comes from your throne, wherever it takes me, in the busyness of the city and in the quietness of the country, in the rushing waters of its rapids as well as in the still pools of water. I want to be in its clear crystal life-giving flow."

Rock

God is your strength in time of trouble

Rock of Ages, cleft for me, let me hide myself in thee (A. M. Toplady).

The Lord is my rock, my fortress, and my deliverer, my God, my rock, in whom I take refuge (2 Samuel 22:2).

We talk about a person being solid as a rock, meaning that the individual is strong and dependable. A person like this can be relied on to support us in a difficult time, and to know what to do when something unexpected happens.

This is the position that God holds in our lives. God stands as a mighty fortress around us when we are embattled. God will protect us from spiritual onslaughts and will provide a place where we can hide while we gain strength for the battle.

Confronted with a difficulty such as an illness, a death, or the loss of a job, we can say to God, as to a friend, "What am I going to do? How am I going to cope?" A friend would stand by us, give an objective piece of advice, hold us and let us cry, perhaps lend us money, help us to get another job, or baby-sit the children while we deal with the difficulty. We might well ask what God can do in such circumstances. Isn't it better to rely on a friend? Didn't God allow the trouble in the first place? Why would God want to help us now?

God does not create pain; pain is part of life. But God can be part of the solution if we allow it. God will send a friend who can help, will support us while we go through the difficulty, and will be our fortress and strength.

Lead me to the rock that is higher than I (Psalm 61:2).

Through times of trial, faith grows stronger, and we are lifted to a higher plateau and a greater understanding of God's love. It is like walking up one of those spiral staircases that are found in old buildings such as castles and towers. As we walk up the stairs, the view from the windows will be of the same landscape, yet the higher we go, the wider will be the outlook, and the greater the expanse of our vision.

Prayer suggestions

- ❧ "Lord, be my rock, my fortress, and my deliverer."
- ❧ "Lead me through my difficulties and trials and on to a higher plateau, a stronger faith."
- ❧ "Thank you for sending the strength and help I need in my time of hardship."
- ❧ "Help me to be ready to be sent by you when others need your strength."

Seed

Seeds of the Spirit
coming to fruition in your life

Listen! A sower went out to sow. And as he sowed, some
seeds fell on the path, and the birds came and ate them up.
Other seeds fell on rocky ground, where they did not have
much soil, and they sprang up quickly, since they had no
depth of soil. But when the sun rose, they were scorched;
and since they had no root, they withered away. Other
seeds fell among thorns, and the thorns grew up and
choked them. Other seeds fell on good soil and brought
forth grain (Matthew 13:3–8).

It isn't easy for seeds to come to fruition. There are many odds
against their survival. Yet some survive and grow and flourish in

spite of all. Seeds that have been eaten by the birds, for instance, may be dropped on the ground in excrement and flourish far from where they were produced. Some seeds grow in hardly any soil, spreading their root system into rocky crevices, such as trees on Canada's Precambrian Shield.

Some years ago I saw a tomato plant growing in front of an apartment building in Toronto. It had pushed its way through a crack in the sidewalk. Against all odds it was growing and producing fruit; despite the adverse conditions it had come to fruition.

God performs this miracle in plants and trees, and God can perform the same miracle in us.

> *Every moment and every event of every man's life on earth*
> *plants something in his soul. For just as the wind carries*
> *thousands of winged seeds, so each moment brings with it*
> *germs of spiritual vitality that come to rest imperceptibly*
> *in the minds and wills of men* (Thomas Merton, New
> Seeds of Contemplation).

We should never give up on anyone — God never does. Even though it may seem impossible for a particular person to change, it does happen. Someone may seem hardened and unable to receive the seed, let alone allow it to grow. But the spirit of God exists in everyone. The seed may have been lying dormant for years, buried under layers of difficult circumstances.

If that seed is warmed by the sun and swelled by the rain of God, through acts of kindness or love, it can put down roots and push up shoots through hard soil. The roots find nourishment in the soul — hidden nourishment, put there long ago by a mother, a teacher, or a friend. The seed grows into a plant with flowers and fruit — beautiful fruit, acts of kindness or love.

> *What you sow does not come to life unless it dies. And as*
> *for what you sow, you do not sow the body that is to be,*
> *but a bare seed, perhaps of wheat or of some other grain.*
> *But God gives it a body as he has chosen, and to each*
> *kind of seed its own body* (1 Corinthians 15:36—38).

We can suffer a long time from seeing ourselves as ugly ducklings or bad apples. Sometimes we need another person to show us who we are before we can realize our true worth and reflect our true identity. God provides sun and rain through the people we meet every day — colleagues, friends, family — so that the seed planted in us may grow.

We in turn can help to mediate God's sun and rain to others. All of us can be the means to help each other grow toward God.

Prayer suggestions

- ∾ "Great Sower of the seed, I give thanks that you have planted your seed in me. Nourish the soil that it may come to fruition in me as you planned."
- ∾ "Great Farmer of the field, I am sorry when I have provided inappropriate conditions for the seed to grow. Help me to see the harvest I am becoming."
- ∾ "Great Cultivator of the earth, let me be sun and rain for others, so that your seed may grow to fruition in them."

Shadow

God's shadow protects you from harm

Shadows are places where unpleasant things may lurk. We expect something to jump out from the shadows and perhaps do us harm. We attempt to avoid dark places. We prefer to walk in well-lit areas where we will be safe.

But shadows can also provide shelter where we hide from harm. And if the shadow is God's shadow, it will offer protection from evil.

You who live in the shelter of the Most High,
who abide in the shadow of the Almighty ...
he will cover you with his pinions,
and under his wings you will find refuge (Psalm 91:1, 4).

The Lord is your keeper;
the Lord is your shade at your right hand,
The sun shall not strike you by day,
nor the moon by night (Psalm 121:5, 6).

The Lord will create ... a cloud by day and smoke and the
shining of a flaming fire by night.... It will serve as a
pavilion, a shade by day from the heat, and a refuge and a
shelter from the storm and rain (Isaiah 4:5, 6).

In these three readings God is portrayed as our protector. As an eagle covers the young with its wings, so God will protect us. As the shade of a tree prevents sunburn, or a pavilion provides shelter from a storm, so God will protect us in times of spiritual fire and storm.

Sometimes we feel that people or circumstances are overprotective; they stifle us and hold us back from freedom. Then we need to break away from the situation. Always we have to ask ourselves whether the shadow is harmful or protective. Is it a shadow where harm lurks, or is it the shadow of God's wings?

Prayer suggestions

∾ Examine the shadows around you — things or events or people — to discern the shadows of good where you can find safety.

∾ Name the shadows that threaten, and commit yourself to God's protection.

∾ Name the shadows that stifle, and offer them to God with a prayer for freedom.

∾ Name the shadows that are eagle's wings, or a tree's shade, or the pavilion that keeps you safe from the storm. Thank God for the protective shadows in your life.

Sickness and Suffering

Can sickness and suffering bring you closer to God?

We ask, "Why does the good God let bad things happen to good people?" When we fall sick, or someone we know falls sick, we ask this question. We say, "Why me? (or why my friend?) I've done everything I could to follow God's way, and now this has happened. I might just as well have not bothered to keep God's laws, if I get punished anyway."

The first assurance we need is that sickness is not punishment from God. Rather, it is part of living on this earth. Sickness and death come to everyone at some time.

> Beloved, do not be surprised at the fiery ordeal that is
> taking place among you to test you, as though something
> strange were happening to you. But rejoice insofar as
> you are sharing Christ's sufferings, so that you may also
> be glad and shout for joy when his glory is revealed
> (1 Peter 4:12, 13).

I sometimes think it's more difficult for people who have experienced little illness in their early years to deal with it when it comes later in life. Those who have encountered sickness in their family members, or who have suffered some congenital problem themselves, are not as apt to see it as some visitation from God but rather as a way of life to be met every day with God's help. Looking in on such a family from the outside, we might be inclined to ask how they handle so much trouble, pain, and suffering with as much grace and faith as they do.

Supporting and caring for others who are ill exposes us to the grace of God that can come through illness, and reduces some of the fear we have of illness. Then, when we ourselves are ill, or a family member or friend is ill, we can turn to God more readily and perhaps even experience the grace of closer companionship with God.

Prayer suggestions

- ∞ "Lord, why do I have to suffer illness?" (Or, "Lord, why does my family or my friend have to suffer illness?")
- ∞ "Great Healer, help me to know your loving support in time of trouble."
- ∞ "Great Healer, I will seek and accept all assistance to be cured and relieved in my time of suffering."
- ∞ "Lord, you suffered agony on the cross; give me strength to bear illness and suffering that cannot be changed."
- ∞ "Lord, let me show your glory and love to all, so that my suffering can be a blessing to others and not a burden."

Signposts
Discerning God's will for your life

From time to time as we walk along the path of life, we reach a fork in the road and we pray for God's guidance to show us the right path.

Sometimes there are signposts — this way, career or volunteer work; that way, family responsibilities; this way, adopt a child; that way, teach basic literacy classes. A decision is more difficult when there are options. We pray and agonize over the situation because we want to make the right choice.

When the choices are about work to be done, we naturally want to find work that suits the talents that God has given us. There is no point in choosing work that involves heavy physical labour if we haven't the bodily strength to do the job. Yet we may feel drawn to a certain task because we know it is difficult; or at any rate, we may feel a little guilty about choosing what appears to be an easier path. But in God's vast vineyard, as big as the whole world, there is plenty of work for everyone, and God's will lies at the end of every road we might follow. If after careful prayer we decide on one thing, and then roadblocks appear at every step of the way, we may do best to let it go. Perhaps God needs something else from us.

In order for God's work to grow we may have to release it. In the beginning God gives us something to do, and we grasp it, giving our whole selves to God's kingdom. But if our hold on the work becomes so tight that God's kingdom begins to wither in our grasp, we need to take a good look at what is happening. Is

God preparing something else for us to do? The gift God gives us has to be shared with others; only then can it grow and be used for building up the kingdom.

> *The flower I held in my hands withered in my hands....*
> *At the turn of the lane the wall rose up before me....*
> *Suddenly between the trees I saw the end of the forest*
> *which I thought had no end. The testing time had come....*
> *But it did not bring me unalleviated sorrow. On the*
> *contrary, a glorious, unsuspected joy invaded my soul*
> (Source unknown).

Prayer suggestions

- ∾ "Lord, let my talents be used for work that gives life to your whole vast vineyard. Let me not grasp the work as if it were mine and not yours. Let me share the labour and its fruits with others."
- ∾ "When it is time to let go of the work, let me remember that you have something else for me to do. Let me be open to the joy that comes from moving on to your next field."

Telling the People
Writing down the story of your journey with Christ

As Christians and as people of prayer, we know that God has done great things for us, and we want to tell others about God's action in our lives. We are witnesses of Christ's continued working in the world through the Holy Spirit.

> *We declare to you what was from the beginning, what we have heard, what we have seen with our eyes, what we have looked at and touched with our hands, concerning the word of life — this life was revealed, and we have seen it and testify to it, and declare to you the eternal life that was with the Father and was revealed to us — we declare to you what we have seen and heard so that you also may have*

fellowship with us; and truly our fellowship is with the
Father and with his Son Jesus Christ (1 John1:1–3).

Each of us came to the spiritual place where we now stand by a
unique route and path. Writing down the story of our own spiritual journey leaves a record for our children, our community,
our church group.

Just as important as the story of an individual's spiritual walk
is the tale of a community's journey with God.

> *It is important that the members of the community*
> *remember together and with the new people who arrive,*
> *what Providence has done for them, and that they give*
> *thanks for it. The history of a community is important. It*
> *should be told and retold, written and repeated. We are so*
> *quick to forget what God has done! We have to remember*
> *time and again that God is at the origin of everything,*
> *and that it is he who has watched lovingly over the*
> *community. Thus it is that we refind the hope and the*
> *boldness we need to take new risks, and accept difficulties*
> *and suffering with courage and perseverance. The whole*
> *of Holy Scripture, as the Jews recognize so well, is a*
> *constant reminder of how God has watched over his*
> *people. It is when we remember this that we find the*
> *confidence to continue without stumbling* (Jean Vanier,
> Community and Growth).

> *Things which we have heard and known,*
> *that our ancestors have told us,*
> *We will not hide from their children.*

we will tell to the coming generations
the glorious deeds of the Lord, and his might,
and the wonders that he has done (Psalm 78:3, 4).

Suggestions for writing about your spiritual journey

As a community

∾ You could get a group together at church to write your own "church psalm," using Psalm 78 as an example.

How did your church get started? Put it in your psalm.
What were the difficulties, the good things? Put them in the psalm.
Have copies printed for all the church members and for visitors to your church.

As an individual

∾ Record your spiritual journey in sections representing about five years each.

Include photos of your christening, confirmation, or wedding.
[Include descriptions of special moments.]
Include prayers that you use in your life.
Have copies printed to give to your family members.
Include some blank pages where further stories about you may be added later.

Thirst

A spiritual desire to know God

As the deer longs for the flowing stream,
so my soul longs for you, O God.
My soul thirsts for God, for the living God.
When shall I come and behold the face of God? (Psalm
42:1, 2).

The thirst described in these verses is a spiritual thirst — a desire to know God. The desire is so strong that it feels as if you are parched from thirst and that, if you don't find God, you will die.

To be without water in your physical body is to die. You can survive many days without food, but you cannot live long without water. For your soul to live, you need spiritual water. Christ tells us that in him is the supply of spiritual water and that, if we drink of him, we will never be thirsty.

While Jesus was standing there, he cried out, "Let anyone
who is thirsty come to me, and let the one who believes in
me drink" (John 7:37–38).

Those who drink of the water that I will give them will
never be thirsty. The water that I will give will become
in them a spring of water gushing up to eternal life
(John 4:14).

When we are distracted and forget to include Christ in our plans, we become thirsty for spiritual drink. We need to drink at the well of life. Busy with our projects and pleasures, we forget that Christ is the creative energy behind all our ideas, the water without which nothing can live and grow. So the projects fail or fall short of what we had hoped, and we lose the energy needed to finish what we started. Sometimes we go to other places to satisfy our need for water, only to discover that it is bitter or murky. We have to return to the spiritual source or ask God to cleanse the water we find.

> *They went three days in the wilderness and found no*
> *water. When they came to Marah, they could not drink*
> *the water of Marah because it was bitter.... [Moses] cried*
> *out to the Lord; and the Lord showed him a piece of wood;*
> *he threw it into the water and the water became sweet*
> (Exodus 15:22, 23, 25).

> *He split rocks open in the wilderness*
> *and gave them drink abundantly as from the great deep.*
> *He made streams come out of the rock,*
> *and caused waters to flow down like rivers*
> (Psalm 78:15, 16).

> *Let everyone who is thirsty come. Let anyone who wishes*
> *take the water of life as a gift* (Revelation 22:17).

Prayer suggestions

∾ "Lord, I am thirsty in my spirit. Let me partake of the spiritual spring of water."

∾ "I thank you, Lord, that you continually quench my spiritual thirst."

Unction

Who has a right to anoint the feet of Christ?

According to the *Concise Oxford Dictionary*, the word *unction* means "anointing with oil or unguent for medical purposes or as a religious rite or ceremonial."

One of the most beautiful passages in the New Testament, to my mind, is the story of the anointing of Jesus' feet by a woman who was a sinner.

> *And a woman in the city, who was a sinner, having learned that he was eating in the Pharisee's house, brought an alabaster jar of ointment. She stood behind him at his feet, weeping, and began to bathe his feet with her tears and to dry them with her hair. Then she continued kissing his feet and anointing them with the ointment* (Luke 7:37–38).

Simon, the Pharisee, was offended by this action and thought to himself that, if Jesus were really a prophet, he would know that this woman was a sinner. The parable that Jesus told Simon in reply shows that he did know who this woman was, and he also knew what Simon was thinking. He was indeed a prophet.

> "A certain creditor had two debtors; one owed five hun-
> dred denarii, and the other fifty. When they could not pay,
> he cancelled the debts for both of them. Now which of
> them will love him more?" Simon answered, "I suppose
> the one for whom he cancelled the greater debt." And
> Jesus said to him, "You have judged rightly" (Luke 7:
> 41–43).

A person who has sinned much, and yet has received forgiveness, will be more appreciative of forgiveness than someone who has sinned only a little. A self-righteous person who thinks he is free of sin will be unable to show appreciation or love because he doesn't know that he needs forgiveness.

> Therefore, I tell you, her sins, which were many, have
> been forgiven; hence she has shown great love. But the one
> to whom little is forgiven, loves little (Luke 7:47).

Jesus compared Simon's actions to those of the woman. Simon didn't wash Jesus' feet, but the woman washed his feet with her tears. Simon didn't greet Jesus with a kiss, but the woman kissed his feet. Simon didn't anoint Jesus' head with oil, but the woman poured perfume on his feet.

Like Simon, we sometimes condemn a good action done by a person whom we judge to be in the wrong. We may also condemn the person who knowingly receives a good action from that "bad" person. We may need to take an honest look in the mirror if we find ourselves judging othes in this way.

After another incident when a woman caught in adultery was brought before Jesus to see what he would do, Jesus tells the scribes and Pharisees, "Let anyone among you who is without sin be the first to throw a stone at her" (John 8:7). No one threw a stone because none of them was perfect. Some of us may be lucky enough that others are not aware of our bad qualities, but no one is perfect. Thank God!

Prayer suggestions

- ∾ "Lord, let me not condemn anyone's good actions."
- ∾ "Lord, let me be ready to forgive as you forgive."
- ∾ "Lord, let me be aware of my sins and accept your forgiveness with appreciation."
- ∾ "Lord, let me show my love of you in loving actions to others."

Unknown Path
Stepping out on God's new path for you

Jesus said, "You know the way to the place where I am going." Thomas said to him, "Lord, we do not know where

you are going. How can we know the way?" Jesus said to
him, "I am the way, and the truth, and the life. No one
comes to the Father except through me" (John 14:4–6).

When life proceeds along its usual course, we may become bogged down in our everyday routine or ensnared in the rat-race. Although we may not like what we do or what our life has become, we are at least in well-known territory. "Better the devil you know than the devil you don't." And so we keep trekking along the road of familiarity, even if it has become a road of despondency.

An unfamiliar path or an unknown way may bring moments of confusion or terror — but these are moments when God can enter your life. God has your attention and can show you miracles.

This is what happened to Moses. He was contented with his life as a shepherd, minding the sheep of his father-in-law, until one day he noticed a burning bush that was not consumed in the flames. Moses stepped aside to see it.

Having got Moses' attention, God laid on him the task of freeing his fellow Israelites from slavery. Moses put up an argument in favour of God sending someone else. He said that, as God very well knew, he had never been any good at public speaking and never would be. But God prevailed and reassured him that God would be with him and would send him all the help he needed.

The Israelites were slaves to the Egyptians, and though life was hard, it was uncomplicated — they went to work, they came home, they had bread on the table. That is, until Moses was sent by God to lead the Israelites out of Egypt. With Moses as their leader, they abandoned their comfortable slavery and strove for a new freedom, but at a cost. They suffered more hardships from Pharoah's hand, pursuit into the Red Sea and, finally, near starvation in the wilderness.

> *They said to Moses, "Was it because there were no graves in Egypt that you have taken us away to die in the wilderness? What have you done to us, bringing us out of Egypt? Is this not the very thing we told you in Egypt, 'Let us alone and let us serve the Egyptians'? For it would have been better for us to serve the Egyptians than to die in the wilderness"* (Exodus 14:11–12).

We know the happy ending: God opened the sea to let the Israelites pass through and then closed it again to drown Pharaoh and all his host. But this triumph was followed by more trials: years of wandering that led to discouragement, complaint, and the near abandonment of the worship of God. The next triumph, the entry into the promised land, brought its own trials. And so the story continues throughout the Old Testament and the New and into our own lives.

Whenever we get too comfortable, God is likely to wake us up. The sound of the alarm is often a brutal assault on our comfort, and we launch out once again into unknown territory. In our stepping out beyond the familiar, God is with us and leading us and, if we are attentive, there comes a moment when we see all this and give thanks.

Prayer suggestions

- ❧ "I am like Thomas, Lord. I say that I don't know where you are going so how can I know the way? But you reply that you are going to prepare a place for me, so that where you are I can be with you. Lord, help me to remember your promise that you are the Way."

- ❧ "I am like Moses, Lord. I say that, as you well know, I've never been good at doing this thing that you are now asking of me. Send someone else to do it — someone qualified, who can do a better job than I. But I know that you are looking for someone through whom you can work, perhaps someone apparently inadequate for the task. I don't have to be qualified — I just have to trust in you."

- ❧ "I am like the Israelites, Lord. I remember the comfort of the good old days, and I complain at the hardships that you have got me into. But I know that, thanks to you, triumphs follow trials. And I know too that the trials draw me back to you, my leader, my guide, my protector."

Vocation

Answering God's vocation

Then I heard the voice of the Lord saying, "Whom shall I send, and who will go for us?" And I said, "Here am I; send me!" (Isaiah 6:8).

This verse of scripture sounds straightforward. God asks if there's anyone willing to do what needs to be done, and Isaiah says that he's here and will do it. However, the preceding verses make clear that it's not this simple.

Isaiah received a glorious vision of God seated on his throne in all his splendour and majesty. The seraphs were praising God with such gusto that the whole place shook with their sound, and the temple was filled with the smoke of their incense. Isaiah's response was fear. Even though he had come to the temple to contemplate God, he didn't really expect to see God. He felt he was unworthy and was convinced that, since he had seen God, he was doomed.

> And I said: "Woe is me! I am lost, for I am a man of
> unclean lips, and I live among a people of unclean lips;
> yet my eyes have seen the King, the Lord of hosts!"
> (Isaiah 6:5).

Isaiah's response is typical of us all. We pray to ask God to show himself and tell us what to do with our lives, and we are confused or frightened when we get an answer. "Who, me?" we say. "Surely you don't mean me? I'm not good enough. I'm not smart enough. I'm scared. You must mean someone else."

God is ready for our excuses. In Isaiah's case, he sent an angel with a live coal taken from the altar. The angel touched Isaiah's lips with the coal and said, "Now that this has touched your lips, your guilt has departed and your sin is blotted out" (Isaiah 6:7). No more excuses! God will decide who is or is not worthy of a particular vocation.

What will he use to convince each one of us of our vocation? A hot coal or a bright light? a disappointment or an overwhelming joy? a rejection or acceptance of our job application? In one way or another, God answers, "This proves it. I mean you. Your reason for not doing it has been taken away. You're the one I want to do this work."

God asks again, "Whom shall I send?" And you answer, "Here I am, send me."

Prayer suggestions

- Ask God what God wants you to do. Don't be surprised if you get a sense of God's presence, or of God's will. If no answer seems to be forthcoming, ask again.

- Be alert to signs of God's answer in the ordinary — or extraordinary — events of life.

- When you think you have heard God's answer, you may not feel that you can do what is being set before you. Say, "Lord, I don't know how to handle this, but if I really must do it, send me the help I need."

- When you are ready say, "Here I am, send me."

Walk with God
Walking with God in faith

Moses said to the Lord, "Now if I have found favour in your sight, show me your ways, so that I may know you and find favour in your sight...." He said, "My presence will go with you, and I will give you rest" (Exodus 33:13, 14).

Sometimes God seems to ask us to go in a new and different direction from the one in which we have previously made a commitment to walk. Perhaps we went into teaching or nursing, and now it seems we should follow some other path, such as that of artist or poet. Perhaps we made vows of marriage or priesthood, and after years of walking this path it seems that we should turn away from it and follow another.

Decisions like these are not easy to make, especially when vows are involved and other people are likely to be hurt. We have to be sure that the decision we make is according to God's will, not just our own whim. Yet we also have to be open to God's guidance, even when this seems to require striking out in a new direction.

Without risk there is no growth. Without growth there is no blossom. To blossom is to take a risk, for to flower is to risk dying. But risk leads to adventure, and with God beside us on the path, every step is a step into life.

Prayer suggestions

- "Lord, I know the path I'm on. I've walked along it with you for many years. It is a sure path. Do you really want me to leave it and walk on a new path?"
- Like your servant Moses, Lord, I pray, "Show me your ways, so that I may know you."
- You said to Moses, "My presence will go with you, and I will give you rest." Lord, I take your hand and walk this new path with you. May it be a path of adventure and a new blossoming.

Water becomes Wine

Allowing Christ to change the water of your life into wine

The story of the first miracle that Jesus performed is recorded in John 2:1–11. It is the miracle of changing water into wine. I think it's wonderful that the first of Jesus' miracles is almost frivolous. It wasn't a miracle of healing or bringing the dead back to life; he didn't cure someone of blindness or make someone walk. His first miracle is done to save someone's wedding feast from disaster.

Jesus and his disciples had been invited to a wedding in Cana of Galilee. Mary, his mother, was also there. Perhaps it was a wedding of relatives or friends of the family. Wedding feasts went on for several days, and when the wine ran out, Jesus' mother went to her son and told him that there was no more wine. It is interesting that she merely stated the situation. She didn't ask him to do anything in particular — a lesson in prayer. "Bring it to the Lord in prayer," the old hymn says.

When Mary told Jesus that there was no more wine, he said, "Woman, what concern is that to you and to me? My hour has not yet come." If I got that kind of answer to a prayer, I might be discouraged. But Mary, who knew her son better than anyone, went to the servants and told them to expect something. Whatever Jesus told them to do, they should do it.

When Jesus told them to fill the large stone jars that were usually filled with water for ceremonial washing, they did so.

This was not out of the ordinary. One wonders how they reacted when they were told to pour some out, not for washing but for drinking, and to take it to the master of the feast. They must have thought they would look pretty foolish when he drank it and asked them what they were doing bringing him water to drink instead of wine.

But the water had become wine — wine so good that the master of the feast remarked to the bridegroom on its quality: "Everyone serves the good wine first, and then the inferior wine after the guests have become drunk. But you have kept the good wine until now."

Meditation

Jesus told the servants to take some of the water and give it to someone else. In order for the water to be changed into wine the servants had to give it away. If they had left the water sitting in the jars it would have remained water. When you meditate on God's word, you learn many things about God and the way God works in your life. This is like being filled with water following Christ's command, "Fill the jars with water." When we offer ourselves to others, then the water becomes wine.

Sometimes you may think that what you have to offer is of poor quality and so, out of embarrassment, you decide not to do anything at all. Nothing is too poor to offer others when it is done in Christ's name. He will use the water you have and change it into wine when you act on his word.

Prayer suggestions

- ❧ "Lord, let your servants fill me with the water of life through prayer, love, and friendship."
- ❧ "Lord, let me, as one of your servants, pour out this water of life for others."
- ❧ "Lord, let the water of life we give to one another be changed into the wine of your choosing by the miracle of your word."

$\mathcal{X}$ – chi:
A symbol for Christ

X, or *chi* in the Greek language, is the first letter of the word *Christ* and was used by early Christians as a symbol for *Christ*. It is why the word *Christmas* is sometimes written as "Xmas."

The "X" may be used in combination with the Greek letter "P" or "rho," which is the second letter in Christ's name. This symbol or icon, called "chi-rho," is often seen in churches, sometimes on the embroidered hanging on the pulpit or lectern.

Another symbol in the church, also from Greek, is the acronym ΙΧΗΤΗΥΣ.

Again you see the "X" for Christ. The whole phrase means "Jesus Christ, God's Son, (Our) Saviour," or in Greek, "Iesous Christos Theou Uios Soter."

The acronym, or first letters of this phrase, gives rise to another symbol, that of the fish. The Greek word *ichthus* means fish and, at the time when the church was suffering persecution, it became the secret sign for Christians.

Prayer suggestions

∽ Use the phrase "Jesus Christ God's Son, Our Saviour," as an act of adoration.

∽ Print out the phrase "Jesus Christ God's Son, Our Saviour," and decorate it with the Christian symbol of the fish. Frame it and put it on your prayer table.

Yeast

Christ works in your life as leaven works in dough

Yeast, like the mushroom, is a plant in the fungus family. In baking, yeast works on the sugars and makes carbon dioxide that causes the dough to rise. In wine or beer making, yeast works on the sugars and turns them into alcohol. It takes only a small amount of yeast to transform a mixture of flour, water, and sugar into a loaf of bread, or a mixture of fruit, water, and sugar into wine.

In the Bible we read of yeast or leaven as an analogy for the kingdom of God.

Jesus said, "To what should I compare the kingdom of God? It is like yeast that a woman took and mixed in with three measures of flour until all of it was leavened" (Luke 13:20–21).

Jesus tells us that one of the ways we experience the coming of God's kingdom is by recognizing the goodness that is already in our own lives. This goodness is Christ in us, gradually making us Christ-like. Christ is the yeast that transforms us into himself.

We received Christ in our baptism, were confirmed in Christ in our confirmation, and renew his life in us in the Eucharist. By the sacraments, by hearing and reading the Bible, by prayer, and by the good things we do, we create the right environment for the leaven of Christ to transform us into people who live the life of the kingdom.

Just as we can allow good to work in us, so we can also allow evil to work in us. St Paul calls this "the old leaven" that we should get rid of.

> *Do you not know that a little yeast leavens the whole*
> *batch of dough? Clean out the old yeast so that you may*
> *be a new batch, as you really are unleavened*
> (1 Corinthians 5:6–7).

Our pioneer forebears kept the leaven from one baking till the next because there were no corner stores where they could easily buy more yeast. Sometimes a request for a portion of this leaven "mother," as it was called, would come from a neighbour whose own leaven had gone bad. These pioneers knew from experience that if bad leaven was used in the dough, the bread would be a disaster. The same thing can happen when you make wine. Wild yeast from the air can spoil the batch. In the same way, the wild yeast of evil can make life distasteful, lacking in joy and love. The pure leaven of Christ is needed to replace it.

Prayer suggestions

- Think of the good things that have happened to you or been done for you this week — or throughout your life. Think of the good that you find when you look into your own heart. Ask God to let this leaven of goodness grow in you.
- Think honestly about the bad things that have happened and the unkindness that you sometimes harbour. Ask Jesus to help you to reject actions that increase the world's store of evil.
- Pray for courage to choose to do what is good. Ask your guardian angel to assist you in making good choices and carrying them out.

Yoke of Christ
Christ as a partner in your life

Come to me, all you that are weary and are carrying heavy burdens, and I will give you rest. Take my yoke upon you, and learn from me; for I am gentle and humble in heart, and you will find rest for your souls. For my yoke is easy, and my burden is light (Matthew 11:28–30).

A yoke is a wooden crosspiece that fits across a person's shoulders so that a bucket or other weight can be hung on either side. Some yokes were designed so that two people could share the weight. To take on the yoke of Christ is to have Christ as a partner who shares the burdens we have to bear. On hard days Christ will pull more than his share of the weight.

This doesn't mean that we aren't to pull our weight too. It is a partnership. When we put on the yoke of Christ, we walk together with him in step. His yoke is easy. It won't rub and chafe but will support us on our way.

Prayer suggestions

∾ "Christ Jesus, my partner in life, let me take on your yoke on my shoulders and walk with you. Let me keep time with you."

∾ "Lord Jesus, with you as my yoke-mate, life is a joyful adventure. You make my heaviest burdens light, and together we can run, dance, and skip."

Zacchaeus

Don't be surprised at God's choice of followers

The story of Zacchaeus found in Luke 19 tells of a man, a chief tax collector, who was as unpopular in the time of Christ as the tax collector is today. In the time of Jesus, taxes paid to the Romans were especially resented because the Romans had conquered the Jewish people and occupied their land. Zacchaeus was particularly disliked because he was not only a tax collector, but he also got rich from the job, and he himself admitted that some of his wealth had come by fraudulent means.

One day, a large crowd gathered to see Jesus walk through Jericho. Zacchaeus was anxious to see who was causing all the excitement. Because he was a short man, he was unable to see over the heads of the people, but he was determined not to miss out on the events. So he ran on ahead, and climbed a sycamore tree to get a good view of all the happenings. When Jesus got to the tree where Zacchaeus was perched, he stopped and looked up. He called the tax collector by name, telling him to hurry and come down because he planned to stay at his house. Zacchaeus, happy that he had been singled out to host Jesus, rushed home to prepare for his visit.

Others in the crowd criticized Jesus for choosing to stop at the house of a sinner — one who made a healthy profit from collecting taxes from his own people and paying them to their conquerors, and had also done a little cheating on the side. Zacchaeus promised at that moment to become a reformed character. He said that he would give half his possessions to the poor and repay four times as much to anybody he had defrauded.

Jesus had called him by name — had given him a chance — and Zacchaeus responded by doing all he could to show that Jesus' trust was justified.

> *Then Jesus said to him, "Today salvation has come to this house, because he too is a son of Abraham. For the Son of Man came to seek out and to save the lost"* (Luke 19:9, 10).

Jesus shows he is willing to forgive those who have done wrong — including us. God is always ready to forgive us, but we have to be ready to receive it. First he finds us, and then he gives us opportunity to repent and change our ways. When the Pharisees attacked him for spending time with sinners and forgiving them, Jesus said:

I tell you, there will be more joy in heaven over one sinner who repents than over ninety-nine righteous persons who need no repentance (Luke 15:7).

The story of Zacchaeus also cautions us to be careful about criticizing other people's morals and behaviour without taking a good look at our own. Jesus forgave the person whom everybody considered to be the worst sinner of all. But Zacchaeus didn't just say he had done wrong; he proposed a plan of action to put things right with the people he had wronged. This is the challenge for us too.

Prayer suggestions

- ❧ "Lord, I see the sin in my own heart. I see reflected there some of what I criticize in others. Will you call me to repentance and forgive me? I am ready to hear your call."
- ❧ "Lord, I see the sin that other people do. Will you call them to repentance and forgive them? I know that I must forgive them too."
- ❧ "Lord, I am sorry for what I have done that hurts you and other people and the Earth. What must I do to put it right? I will do what I can."
- ❧ If at the moment you are not aware of anything hurtful that you have done, say, "Lord, thank you for all the times when you have protected me and kept me from sin. Help me to be forgiving of those who have strayed from your path.

Path Books
A LIGHT TO MY PATH

We hope that you have enjoyed reading this Path Book. For more information about Path Books, please visit our website at **www.pathbooks.com**. If you have comments or suggestions about Path Books, please write to us at **publisher@pathbooks.com**.

Other Path Books

The Habit of Hope: In a Changing and Uncertain World by William Hockin. Wise and friendly guidance to help people living in an age of confusion and change to transform personal experience in the light of biblical story.
1-55126-325-4 $14.95

Practical Prayer: Making Space for God in Everyday Life by Anne Tanner. A richly textured presentation of the history, practices, and implications of Christian prayer and meditation to help people live a rewarding life in a stressful world.
1-55126-321-1 $18.95

Also available: *Prayer: Leader's Resources*, a booklet for study groups, and *Practical Prayer: An Exercise in Contemplative Prayer*, a cassette tape on meditation practice.

Available from your local bookstore or
Anglican Book Centre, phone 1-800-268-1168
or write 600 Jarvis Street, Toronto, ON M4Y 2J6